Possessing Your
Accolades

"Commit your works unto the Lord, and He will establish your thoughts."
Proverbs 16:3. Another translation says—"and He will guarantee your success."
I like that even better! The point is this: God created everything there is and
wants man to be successful in his stewardship of creation. Rodney Johnson has
tapped into that wonderful truth, and shares it with us in very practical ways, from
his own experience. What could be better?

—PAT BOONE
Legendary recording artist, actor, best-selling author, and entrepreneur

My longtime friend, Rodney Johnson, is not only an expert in Southern
California real estate, but a man who strives to serve God's purpose in every deal
he closes.
   Does it matter to God where you live? This book will be a vivid reminder that
the God who birthed life on planet Earth is still interested in making homes for
His people on it.

—DEAN JONES
Actor, President/Founder Christian Rescue Committee

Rodney Johnson's book, Possessing Your Promised Land: Biblical Principles
for Real Estate Acquisition *is a read that will inspire, educate, and guide you*
through any real estate transaction. Our Lord said, "I came that you might have
life and have it more abundantly." Rodney explains God's word and how your
mindset translates into acquiring real estate properties—among other things—
according to God's plan. It's a MUST READ—and it's all biblical!

—GAVIN MACLEOD
Actor, *The Love Boat* and *The Mary Tyler Moore Show*

Rodney Johnson's Possessing Your Promised Land *shows the reader firsthand*
how to develop a mindset geared toward acquiring real estate.   His exciting
examples culled from almost twenty years of helping people "possess their own
promised lands" make this an enjoyable read. If God has been nudging you to
step out into the unknown like He called Abraham to do then, by all means, read
this book.

—PAUL MCGUIRE
Best-selling author & Syndicated Talk Show Host of
The Paul McGuire Show

From the political to the practical, Rodney Johnson covers it in Possessing Your Promised Land. *Whether it is using his garage as a polling site in national elections or taking the appropriate tax deduction, he has something to say that should be of benefit to all homeowners and those who want to be homeowners. This book is not about "mansions in the sweet by and by." Instead, Rodney uses biblical examples and characters to show us what we need to do in the "here and now." I encourage you to read* Possessing Your Promised Land *and then do what the title suggests.*

—MICHAEL REAGAN
Radio talk show host of the nationally syndicated *The Michael Reagan Show* and author of the bestselling book, *Twice Adopted.*

Rodney Johnson has performed a unique service for both Christians and non-Christians alike in this immensely readable and inspiring book. His fresh and insightful application of Biblical truth to the subject of real estate ownership places the concept of "possessing the land" in a context that is compelling and relevant to everyday life in the 21st century. Plus his stories are very funny and enjoyable to read!

—COLIN STEWART
President of the Center for a Just Society Washington, DC,
Former VP of the Family Research Council

Rodney Johnson has a great and practical grasp of those important biblical principles which lead people into victorious living. Through actual case studies of people living today as well as those living during biblical times, he shows the reader the greatness of God's promises while, at the same time, evidencing the very real challenges everyone seemingly faces while living in an imperfect world.

Rodney Johnson lives a Spirit-filled life. Through this tremendous series of true stories, he seeks to help others appropriate the full potential of God's intentions for us all. Rodney is loving and engaging in his instructiveness, leaving no room for casual religious living. His is an active Christian life that works!

—JIM TOLLE
Senior Pastor, The Church on the Way, Van Nuys, CA

Possessing Your Promised Land *is full of hope, faith and encouragement to believe your real estate dreams really can come true. Rodney Johnson provides all that plus the practical direction to make it happen. Above all, this unique and timely book reminds us that if we delight in God then He gives us the desires of our hearts, and it is God's heart-desire to give us a home—both earthly and heavenly!*

—LISA WHELCHEL
Author of the bestsellers *Creative Correction* and *The Facts of Life and Other Lessons My Father Taught Me,* and founder of *MomTime Ministries.*

POSSESSING *YOUR* PROMISED LAND™

Biblical Principles for
Real Estate Acquisition

H. Rodney Johnson
REALTOR®

Paradigm™
Seed Publishers, Inc.
www.pspublishers.com

If you purchased this book without a cover, you need to be aware that it is likely a copy that was fraudulently reported to the publisher as unsold or destroyed. Consequently, you may have purchased stolen property since neither the publisher, nor the author, have received any payment for this stripped book. We hope that this notice will persuade you to avoid contributing to the errors of those who have chosen to act illegally.

This publication has been written with the intention of providing competent and reliable information concerning the subject matter covered. Nevertheless, it is sold with the express understanding that neither the author nor publisher are engaged in rendering specific legal, financial, or other professional advice regarding the reader's specific situation and circumstances. Laws and professional practices differ from state to state and country to country in most instances. If legal, professional, or expert assistance is required, the services of a qualified professional should be sought in your area. The author and publisher specifically deny and disclaim any liability, loss, or risk that is incurred as a consequence, directly or indirectly, of the application and use of the contents of this book.

Actual accounts are used within this book, based on the author's own recollection of the events that occurred. However, the names have been changed or omitted and some details excluded or altered, for both educational purposes and to protect the anonymity of other people involved. Any similarities of events herein described to the stories or testimonies of others not personally known to the author are purely coincidental.

The leaf logo and Paradigm Seed Publishers, Inc. logo are trademarks of Paradigm Seed Publishers, Inc. of Fort Worth, Texas.

"Possessing Your Promised Land" and "TRINSPIRATION" are trademarks of Refreshing Productions, Inc. of Chatsworth, California.

REALTOR® is a registered trademark of THE NATIONAL ASSOCIATION OF REALTORS®

Fine Homes and Estates® is a registered trademark of CENTURY 21 Real Estate Corporation.

Unless otherwise stated, all Scripture citations are taken from the New King James Version. Copyright © 1982 by Thomas Nelson, Inc. Used by permission. All rights reserved.
All Scripture citations marked "NIV" are taken from the HOLY BIBLE, NEW INTERNATIONAL VERSION®. Copyright © 1973, 1978, 1984 International Bible Society. Used by permission of Zondervan. All rights reserved.
All Scripture citations marked "AMP" are taken from the Amplified® Bible, Copyright © 1954, 1958, 1962, 1964, 1965, 1987 by The Lockman Foundation Used by permission. (www.Lockman.org)

International Standard Book Numbers:
1-933141-03-4 (perfect bound)
1-933141-04-2 (e-Book edition)

Copyright ©2005 by H. Rodney Johnson
All rights reserved. Written permission must be secured from the publisher to use or reproduce any part of this book, in any form, except for brief quotations in critical reviews or articles.

Published by Paradigm Seed Publishers, Inc. of Fort Worth, Texas.
Visit us at www.pspublishers.com for more information, and news regarding upcoming new title releases. Join our online newsletter list for advanced updates on new releases and special events.

Cover design by Neal Brown and Rich Vermillion.

Dedication

I never would have started in the real estate field, let alone continued in it or become successful, without the support and mentoring of my father-in-law, Harold Dyck. You taught me how to make a listing presentation. You taught me what to say when a client stumped me with a question. You were, and will always remain, available to give your advice—when asked for it. Dad, you said that you have never found another man whom you would rather have for a son-in-law. Well, I have never found another man I would rather have for a father-in-law. So we're even. By the way, I am glad you are not looking for my replacement. I will be over for dinner and let's watch one of those 50-plus Bill Gaither videos you have in your collection.

About the Author

Rodney Johnson is a gifted writer, speaker, worship leader, and veteran of the real estate industry for nearly twenty years. An experienced real estate broker, Rodney has been personally involved in property transfers totaling well-over a hundred million dollars. He has been the top CENTURY 21 Fine Homes and Estates™ agent in California's San Fernando Valley since 2001 and, at the time of this writing, has achieved "Top Producer" status for the last three years in the 120-agent firm he is a part of. Rodney has also been featured on HGTV's number one rated television program, "House Hunters." As extensive as these professional real estate credentials are, Rodney also serves his industry as a coach to other real estate professionals.

As a believer in the marketplace, Rodney has been privileged to represent many Christian (and non-Christian) individuals and families in their real estate pursuits. Furthermore, he has also represented major denominations, colleges, seminaries, churches, pastors, evangelists and other ministries in their relocation projects, property sales, and purchases. He is also a member of the fast-growing national and international Christian business organization— the ProVision Network (www.provisionnetwork.org).

A talented author, Rodney was previously published as a contributor to Stormie Ormartian's *The Power of a Praying®️ Husband*. Part of Rodney's personal testimony was also profiled in Rebecca Hayford Bauer's book, *Seasons of Praise*. His song, "We Applaud Your Greatness," was released on the Hosanna Integrity project, *Men in Worship with Jack Hayford*. In his book, *Experiencing God Together*, Dr. David Stoop quoted the lyrics to Rodney's song as he recounted his congregation's experience with God, singing its worshipful phrases together.

Rodney and his wife, Valerie, live in California and enjoy three marvelous children together. The Johnson clan calls The Church on the Way in Van Nuys, California their home church, where Rodney continues to serve as one of five rotating worship leaders.

Acknowledgments

Building a successful real estate business is a team effort. First and foremost, I would like to acknowledge my team: Robynn Creitz has been a faithful assistant since 1993, and in the last three years has become a great buyer's agent for us in the Santa Clarita Valley. My mother-in-law, Etheline Dyck, chose to come back into the work place in 1994 after the Northridge earthquake to help out two days a week to keep continuity in my business. For that I am grateful. Joseph Cadicamo stepped out into the unknown in 1999, joining our team, and has become a gifted real estate investor in his own right. Your best years are ahead of you, Joseph. Thank you team for your generosity, prayers and support.

For over eighteen years, I have called CENTURY 21 All Properties, Inc. my real estate home base. I have stayed there because of the support from Rich Miller, Edward Wankovsky, Joe Andrews, and Tom Morehouse. Thanks guys.

My spiritual team consists of key pastors and members of The Church on the Way, Van Nuys, California. Pastor Jack Hayford's keen insights into the Word of God have caused my spiritual development to flourish. It continues to blossom under the teaching of our new senior pastor, Jim Tolle. Dr. Scott Bauer's friendship also played a significant role in my growth before his home going in 2003. John Houghton's discipleship of men at our church was vital in my becoming both a spiritual and business leader.

To Rich Vermillion, thank you for your patience in the writing of this book and for your guidance in making it better. To Mr. Grammarian, Bill Creitz, thanks for your proofreading, being an extraordinary editor, and just all around good friend. Bill Meck, you made me look good through your camera lens.

To Gaylon TeSlaa, Joseph Cadicamo, Christopher Riley, and Amick Byram thanks for the Wednesday morning prayer times. Your support was pivotal in the birthing of this book. To my email prayer team, thanks for undergirding this project with your faithful prayers.

To Team Family—the prayers of my sister, Ronda; niece, Ashlie; and my parents, Hal and Fern Johnson, mean more to me than you will ever know. Thanks to Ralph for allowing me to represent you in my very first closing in 1987, and for continuing to use me throughout the years. You are a great brother-in-law. Thanks to my other brother-in-law, Mark, for helping us with our first fixer-upper. You are a master craftsman.

R.J., as a three year old, you used to send me off to work with the admonition, "Get a listing, Daddy." As an elementary school student, you prayed for a house with a big backyard and a swimming pool. God answered your prayers, son, and will continue to do so. Continue to dream big, R.J., and pursue those dreams aggressively. Emily, you are coming into your own as a young woman of God. Whether you are on a sandy beach or a wood volleyball court, remember that you can do all things through the One who strengthens you. Kelly's soccer coach tells her to find some real estate and "put an address on it," by kicking to an open player. I want to be standing on a piece of world famous real estate in 2012 watching you win the gold medal for the U.S. Soccer team. I love all three of you kids.

Valerie, you always support me when I say, "Let's make an offer on this piece of real estate." Having you as my wife has made it all worthwhile. You are the best.

POSSESSING YOUR PROMISED LAND™

Contents

Foreword
by Pastor Jack Hayford

To commend H. Rodney Johnson's work in *Possessing Your Promised Land* to readers is a remarkable point of rejoicing for me. First, because Rodney is so skilled at what he does as a businessman; then because he is so professionally thorough in every enterprise he pursues; and third because he is so consistent in his life as a man of character, of deep family commitment and of Christian living and service.

However, it is also very moving for me because of my relationship with him and his wife, Valerie, through the years of serving as their pastor at The Church on the Way. Paul spoke of Timothy as "a true son in the faith," and without hesitation, I readily express the same of Rodney Johnson. The information you discover in this remarkable piece of work has been hammered out on the anvil of experience and tempered in the fires of trial. Success does not leap into a person's lap; it comes through hard work, faith and—when a person's "faith" is more than merely in themselves but in Christ—with divine blessing.

Within these pages, Rodney has provided the Body of Christ an exquisite tool with which to begin the task of obeying our Lord's command in Luke 19:13 to "occupy until I come." Most pragmatically interpreted, the Greek verb used here literally refers to "buying and selling"—an insight worthy of note as you take up this book. Herein, Rodney points the way to lay hold of significant biblical keys that will enable your taking possession of actual lands and houses. Nothing could be more practical for anyone, and no one is a more verified tutor or aide in such personal and business pursuits than Rodney.

Simultaneously, Rodney entertains and informs us with his colorful, and sometimes miraculous, real estate experiences. They are wonderful testimonies—and some of them are events I have personally shared with him and Valerie as we rejoiced in God's grace and goodness, when His blessing became distinctly evident.

Just as the writer has verified himself as a valuable partner and

1

servant in our church, I think that you will likewise find him one as he assists you. Read *Possessing Your Promised Land* thoroughly, thoughtfully and prayerfully. Most of all, apply what Rodney so adeptly conveys throughout its pages to your real estate transactions and ambitions, and I believe you will likewise find yourself possessing *your* "Promised Land."

—Dr. Jack W. Hayford, President, International
Foursquare Churches; Chancellor, The King's Seminary;
Founding Pastor, The Church on the Way

Publisher's Biographical Note[1]: A prolific and best-selling author, Pastor Hayford has himself penned more than three dozen books, and 600 hymns and choruses—including the internationally known and widely recorded "Majesty." He is perhaps best known, however, as founding pastor of The Church on the Way (TCOTW), the First Foursquare Church of Van Nuys, California. His service to TCOTW, which began as a temporary assignment to pastor 18 people in 1969, continued fruitfully for more than three decades as the congregation grew to more than 10,000 active members.

For more information concerning the ministry of this "Pastor of pastors," visit any of the following web sites: www.livingway.org, www.kingscollege. edu, and www.kingsseminary.edu.

[1] Derived primarily from information published in Pastor Jack Hayford's full biography on the web site: www.livingway.org. Used with permission.

Introductory Thoughts

As you move forward into the pages of this book, I believe it will be of tremendous benefit to you if you bear in mind a few thoughts. For your convenience, I have assembled them here in the form of brief statements to stimulate your thinking on several key points.

First, God really wants you to own real estate. I believe that with my whole heart. From the first real estate transaction in Genesis when God created the Garden of Eden and leased it to the man and woman to superintend its development, it is obvious that He had homes and land on His mind. Granted, Adam and Eve did not sign a lease agreement; however, they did agree verbally to His contract. In essence, the Landlord, God, told the tenants, Adam and Eve, that he was giving them an option on planet earth. Their part was to take care of the plants and animals. In exchange, they would be wonderfully and gloriously provided with everything they could ever want or need. The only way they could break this lease option was to eat fruit from one forbidden tree in the Garden. We all know what happened—they broke the lease and history has never been the same.

In between the signposts of Genesis and Revelation, we're exhorted to rule and reign on this planet called earth. In fact, the word "land" is used 1,733 times in 1,496 verses in the Bible. The word "house" is used 2,011 times in 1,689 verses. Throughout the book of Revelation, the Bible's final apocalyptic chronicle, real estate is mentioned numerous times. There is a new heaven, a new earth, and a new Jerusalem promised in its pages. Are you beginning to see that God has real estate on His mind?

Our Lord does not appear to have a problem with beautiful buildings, either. The reason He would not let King David build Him a temple was because of David's heart attitude. You see, he was not allowed to build a place of worship because he was a man of war. Solomon, David's son, asked for wisdom instead of great riches and lands. In return, he was allowed to build the temple worth billions in today's economy. He was also given wealth beyond measure and a kingdom of splendor. Let's ask for God's wisdom regarding the lands He would have for us and see what wonderful surprises He has in store.

Have you heard? The three most important rules of real estate are location, location, location. You have been placed in a strategic location by your Creator with a mission to accomplish. Owning and controlling property many times plays a pivotal role in seeing your mission successfully completed. I am approaching the subject of real estate acquisition from a Christian and biblical perspective. Nevertheless, whether you believe the Bible or not, what I say in this book will work for anyone who applies these principles. The reason they will work is simple—"truth is truth."

I have been a student of personal development for more than two decades and have studied the writings of men and women of all faiths and beliefs. Some of them knowingly credit the Bible, while others are not necessarily aware of the source of truth they are teaching. One of the pre-eminent motivational trainers of this era has eaten many Thanksgiving and Christmas dinners at my home. He is quick to credit the Bible as a primary source for many of the lessons he teaches to sold-out crowds around the world. He does it in a way that is non-offensive to the person who is still finding his way regarding faith. I hope to do the same thing in this book, although I do anticipate challenging everyone's comfort zone regarding their mindset as it relates to real estate.

If the thought that God has property for you seems incongruous or incredible, consider this: God gave the children of Israel their own "Promised Land." Not only that, He helped them to miraculously "take the land" and possess it. Then He divided it up tribe-by-tribe and clan-by-clan. In Hebrews, we learn that the new covenant is even better than the first covenant. So, if God had lands and houses for His people in the Old Testament, wouldn't it make sense that those who live under the New Testament could expect the same thing from their covenant?

⁓⇝⇜⁓

For my female readers, I have good news for you. We see in the distribution of land that the daughters of Zelophehad were given their own plot—something that was unheard of in this patriarchal society. Moses was so amazed at their request that He went before God who told Him, "The Daughters of Zelophehad speak what is right. You shall surely give them a possession among their father's brothers, and cause the inheritance of their father to pass to them." Whoa dude, women land owners in the old covenant. Think about the ramifications of that. There's another passage about women landowners that I will discuss later.

⁓⇝⇜⁓

Abraham, the Father of the Faith, is a person Jews and Christians alike can relate to. We will examine his life and how God told him to come out from his father's house and come to a land that God would show him. We'll see all of the changes he had to go through in order to possess his promised land.

In the New Testament, the early church experienced disastrous and deadly results from the real estate deal of two of its members, Ananias and Sapphira. Shortly after the church was birthed on the Day of Pentecost, believers in and around Jerusalem began selling their property and bringing the proceeds to the apostles to be shared in common by all. This husband and wife team decided to sell their land and give some, but not all, of the proceeds to the church. Their mistake was not in holding back a portion of the money. No one was compelling them to sell. However, by claiming that their gift represented all of the profits from the sale, they both died immediately upon confession of this lie to the apostles.

I bring up this Bible story here for two reasons: First, when we get to the chapter about building your real estate team, you will learn why you need to find reliable, honest people whom you can trust. It is vitally important if you want God's blessing on your real estate deals (verses His judgment) that you and those who advise you are completely honest. However, we'll cover more on that later.

The second reason I brought this story up here is because it was recently pointed out to me that, as a result of the first believers selling all of their real estate assets, they later became financially dependent upon the generosity of other believers from Philippi and Corinth. Chapters eight and nine of the second epistle to the Corinthians detail how the Apostle Paul collected a gift from the Corinthian and Macedonian churches to take back to the believers in Jerusalem. (We'll see the importance of giving in the chapter, *How to Get Everything You Want*).

I do not want to ruffle the feathers of our beloved pastors, so please hear my heart when I say, "Nowhere in scripture do I see a command to sell all of your property and give it to the church." Consider this: If the early Christians had rented out those properties, they could have supported themselves adequately while helping the Church financially with the mission works that Peter, Paul, John and others were doing. Instead, they became a financial burden to the Corinthian and Philippian believers.

Let me note for a moment that those of you who are considering a charitable remainder trust (by which you give a piece of property to a charity and continue to retain some of the income from it until your death) I salute you for your generosity. Also, for those of you reading this who feel that God is specifically directing you to sell a property and give the proceeds to your church or some ministry—by all means obey God and do it. I am not really addressing you if you fit into one of these two (or similar) categories.

Instead, by pointing out this issue, I simply want to challenge the mindset that says we should be poor and just "barely get along" in our humble cottage. Rather than unloading everything we have out of some religious misconception of Scripture, we need to learn how to use our assets to produce passive income streams that can finance God's work in perpetuity. Think for just a moment of all of the positive things that we could accomplish for ourselves and for others if we had the mindset, "Money works for me. I do not work for money." Wealthy people who employ money as a servant—with the right heart—can help advance the Gospel farther than those who are themselves slaves to deficiency. That is why the Corinthian and Philippian churches were able to give and be a blessing, while the Jerusalem church had to be supported. Their ill-advised (although good-intentioned) act of property liquidation ultimately positioned them to need financial assistance—despite the abundant wealth of spiritual treasures they certainly did possess.

Finally, for obvious reasons, the names of my clients have been changed to protect their privacy. The infamous ones have been changed to protect me from a lawsuit.

Now that I have given you some food for thought, I invite you to come along as we begin our journey into *Possessing Your Promised Land.*

CHAPTER 1

Supernatural Adventures in Real Estate

In 1996, the tax laws governing the sale of a person's principal residence were different than they are today. Before the current law went into effect, if a couple sold their home, they had two years to re-invest their profit, otherwise they would be taxed on the gain from the sale of their house—to the tune of 40 percent if you combined federal and state penalties! Such was the case with long-time friends, Mitch and Tracy Hargitay.

On March 15, 1994—less than two months after an earthquake measuring 6.8 on the Richter scale had assaulted Southern California—the Hargitays closed escrow on the sale of the home they had lived in for the previous 17 years. Because of the earthquake, displaced homeowners were grabbing the prime rental homes while their houses were being repaired. And due to the lack of inventory, rents were skyrocketing. It was in this climate that Mitch and Tracy took a rental in Sherman Oaks, California, and began to aggressively pursue Mitch's burgeoning composing career. Microphones, computers, mixing boards, keyboards, and cables were just some of the gear that Mitch needed to break into the "ol' boy's club" of composers here in Los Angeles. His investment began to pay off over the next two years. Jobs began coming in. Unfortunately, most of the equity from their home evaporated over the ensuing 21 months, as credit cards were paid off, new equipment was purchased for the home studio and usurious rents were paid.

In January 1996, Mitch approached me and said that we should start the process of finding him and Tracy a home. If they didn't re-invest, they would owe the Internal Revenue Service (IRS) $40,000 in capital gains. At that time, the IRS rules stated that you must buy a home and *be living in it* no later than two years to the day that you had closed on your previous sale. In other words, I had until March 15, 1996, to find them a house that they could be occupying. There was no leeway in this rule, either. The $40,000 penalty hung heavy over our heads. Being the discerning REALTOR® that I am, I began questioning them as to what their needs were. With two kids still living at home, three bedrooms were an absolute minimum. Mitch needed space away from the rest of the house to set up his studio. And Tracy, who is a studio singer and vocal coach, needed a room to call her own, as well. Okay, that was the easy part. Now my next question concerned financing: how much cash did they have for the down payment? Okay, next question.

It seems there was promise of a composing gig that would bring in about $7,000 and they would get back their $4,500 deposit when they moved out of the rental. Not bad; however, when you have to spend a minimum of $240,000 on your new home, the lender wanted to see a minimum $24,000 down from their own funds.

With approximately two months to find a house, arrange financing, close and move into it, we began our search. In very short order, the lender that the Hargitays were working with told them that due to their self-employed status and their lack of a 20 percent down payment, they would need to find a seller who could also carry a second mortgage for them.

Okay, no problem.

"We've got to find a house with three bedrooms, a space for a studio, a seller who is willing to carry a second note on the property *and* be willing to move by March 15," I said under my breath.

January drew to a close and we still hadn't found a house that met the above criteria. I reminded Mitch that we should be starting to make offers no later than the first week of February, as most sellers require 30 to 45 days to move out of their homes. Meanwhile, the lender continued to try to find financing for them. Toward the middle of February, we finally found a house in the heart of the San

Fernando Valley that could work and made an offer. Before accepting our offer, the seller wanted to look at homes for sale in a retirement community. In short order they decided that they couldn't make a decision that quickly and be moved out by March 15. We informed them that they could live in half of the house for a week or two if they needed it, as long as someone from the Hargitay household was living there too. No go. (Hey, desperate times call for desperate measures).

I Have Heard of Rebellious Teenagers, But a Rebellious House?

The next home we found that could work was in North Hollywood, an enclave in the southeast section of the Valley; however, the seller said that in no way could they be moved in less than 30 days. (It was now past the fifteenth of February). With less than a month to go, the pressure was mounting daily.

I would like to say that all of us continued to do what the Apostle Peter admonished and that was to "cast all of your care" on God. Each of us found ourselves casting our cares and then taking them back from time to time. One morning, as I was praying about the Hargitay's need to find a house, I was prompted to turn to the second chapter of Ezekiel. Not being acquainted with that particular chapter, I was anticipating what the Lord would speak to me. It is a short chapter—only ten verses in length. And the first thing the Lord spoke to my spirit after reading the entire chapter was that He was going to do a quick work. That was confirming to me, especially since we had less than 30 days left to see this through to completion. The next thing that caught my attention was verses five and six:

> As for them, whether they hear or whether they refuse—for they are a *rebellious house*—yet they will know that a prophet has been among them. And you, son of man, do not be afraid of them nor be afraid of their words, though briers and thorns are with you and you dwell among scorpions; do not be afraid of their words or dismayed by their

looks, though they are a *rebellious house*. (Italics mine)

I called Mitch and read him the word that the Lord had given me, and suggested that perhaps God was telling us that He was going to use them as redemptive agents in the home that they would purchase. Maybe some type of rebellion had happened there and God needed us to be aware of it. Nevertheless, He was also promising to do a quick work, which we desperately needed.

Bless Tracy's heart. I would call her daily with new listings and say, "Drive by these and tell me if you want to see the inside." She must have looked at more than 80 houses. Toward the end of February, we experienced another blow when the lender that they were working with said that he couldn't find them financing. He suggested that we look elsewhere. Turning to my wife's cousin, Garrett, who had taken an application from other clients of mine on one Friday and closed the following Friday, I asked him to step in and perform the impossible again. He gladly accepted the assignment and set out to find them a loan. Fortunately, work had started coming in for Mitch. He got an advance on a composing gig, some more work materialized and some family members helped cover the remainder of the 10 percent down payment. However, we had one small problem—no house with a studio and no seller who would carry a second mortgage and the requirement that they move in less than 15 day's time. Other than that, we were in fine shape.

When we made the first offer, the listing agent recognized that I had *motivated* buyers with a capital "M" and thus he began calling me about his other listings that might work for the Hargitays. We looked far and wide throughout the San Fernando Valley of over one million residents because time was ticking away. One such listing that he had was in Woodland Hills, on the southwest side of the Valley. We looked at it but the floor plan didn't work. However, the owner of this property told his agent about a friend he had in the north valley who was thinking about moving.

On Thursday night, the seventh of March, one week from D-Day, I showed them another home in Woodland Hills that I thought would *have* to work. As of the next morning, we would have exactly one week to finalize the sale, open escrow, do a physical inspection and termite inspection, get an appraisal, sign loan documents, fund the loan, record the grant deed with the county recorder and be moved in by Friday night. Sounds like a job for Super Agent. Actually, it sounded like a job for a miracle worker, which is what we needed— a miracle!

So back to the house in Woodland Hills. I was ready to write an offer on it as soon as we stepped outside the house; however, Mitch and Tracy didn't want to rush into buying this house without first praying about it.

Reluctantly, I headed for home. The next morning I called Mitch who informed me that they sensed the house was just not right for them. Shaking my head in disbelief, I hung up the phone only to have it ring almost immediately. It was Bernie, the listing agent who had been trying to help me find the Hargitays a house. He told me that he had taken a single party listing the night before for my buyers and asked if they would like to see the house in the north valley. It sounded perfect. To begin with, the owners had just completed all of the earthquake repairs on the main house and were living in the guesthouse out back. Whoa, did I hear the magic words: guest house and vacant main house? The only catch was that it was about $85,000 higher than they needed to spend. I first called Garrett who told me that he could approve them for the higher loan amount, as long as we had a private party carrying a second mortgage. When I described the house to Tracy, she thought it sounded perfect, however, Mitch was skeptical and asked her why she was even going to look at it. "Well, let's see Mitch. If we do not buy a house by next week, we owe the IRS $40,000. I would say let's explore all of our options," Tracy replied. So off we went.

Finding Their Dream Home

When we pulled up in front of the house, a nicely landscaped lawn greeted us. As we stood in front of the newly installed leaded glass door, a sense of anticipation hung in the air. Could this be *the* house, after all of this time looking? God's word about doing a "quick work" would certainly apply here. The owner greeted us and let us in. "Pristine" and "perfect" are two words that come to mind. Tracy's sense that this was *her* house was immediate. God so deeply touched her she began to silently weep as we walked through the house. The kitchen had all new oak cabinets with tile counters and new built-in appliances. Throughout the rest of the house were oak wood floors, French doors, vaulted ceilings, solid core doors, oak moldings, three bedrooms, two-and-a-half bathrooms in the main house *and* a room for Tracy to set up her vocal studio. So far so good. Attached to the main house was a two-car garage. But that was not all. The owner had a business that required another three-car detached garage with a second story that would be perfect for Mitch's studio. Its location away from the house would allow Mitch to stay up until three in the morning scoring movies without disturbing anyone. The "piece de resistance" was a large pool. Tracy was on the phone immediately to Mitch while I began to write the offer.

Even though Mitch was meeting with a producer about a film score, he brought the man with him and decided right on the spot that this was the house for them. Everything else we had seen throughout the previous two months paled in comparison. This was *the* house and all of us knew it—including the seller. The reason he had signed a one-party contract to sell was that his business was located in the north Valencia business park in the Santa Clarita Valley and he wanted to be closer to his work, as well as put his children in the Valencia school system.

As soon as we finished signing off on the purchase contract on the hood of their car, I rang the doorbell and proceeded to present the offer to the listing agent and the sellers. I explained how perfect their property was for the Hargitays in every way and how we could also fulfill the letter of the law by having them move into the *vacant* front house while they continued to live in the studio in back. As I recall, we gave them 30 days of rent-free living while they were looking for a home in Valencia. Our offer also asked them to carry a second mortgage for the Hargitays, as was being required by our lender.

It was at this point in the negotiations that the seller informed me that he had obtained a Small Business Administration (SBA) loan in the amount of $90,000 to repair his home after the earthquake.

14

Moreover, it was at an incredibly low fixed interest rate of 3.9 percent. He wondered out loud if he would be allowed to move the loan to his new property. Neither the listing agent nor I would make any guarantees, although I did volunteer that I had just recently had a client do the very thing he was suggesting.

They asked me to step outside while they considered our offer. When I was called back inside, I was presented with a counter offer that was $10,000 higher than what we had originally offered and the seller made the stipulation that under no circumstances would he be willing to carry a second mortgage. Junior financing would have to be found elsewhere. I presented the counter to Mitch and Tracy and suggested that all three of us start contacting every person we knew to see if we could find someone to carry the second loan.

I went back to my office and began combing through my Rolodex to see who would be willing to provide the secondary financing. On Saturday afternoon, one of the agents in my office said that she had a client who did this sort of thing but that he would want 12 percent as an interest rate for five years. While that seemed high to all three of us, we concluded that we weren't in a position to be bargaining at this point. So without a written agreement from this mysterious investor, we met at our church that evening to sign the counter offer.

Let's Get "Organ-ized"

I must digress a moment and tell you that our church is The Church on the Way in Van Nuys, California. As of this writing, I have been a member there for 24 years and Mitch and Tracy have been members even longer than I. All three of us are involved in the music department, and I was scheduled to play the organ that night. The organ was equipped with a brown phone that would allow me to communicate with the person running the sound equipment. One Sunday in early February before we had found the house, Tracy saw me sitting at the console talking on the phone to the sound man. She quipped to the person sitting beside her that I was her real estate agent and that I was trying to find her a home even while playing the organ. She was expounding on the virtues of my persistence, which she didn't know we would need in only a matter of days. Well, back to our story.

After the service, the three of us met in the side foyer and signed the counter offer. Mitch and Tracy told me that they had asked God for an interest rate on the second loan of no more than 10 percent. I scooted off to the house to deliver the signed contract to the seller. They weren't home, so I left a message on their answering machine congratulating them on the sale of their home. We had found the financing and were ready to close the following Friday.

The Dream House Turns Into a Nightmare

The next morning my telephone rang at home and it was the seller. He informed me that I had not communicated acceptance to him prior to 7 p.m. on Saturday evening; therefore, he considered the contract null and void. Technically, he could do this. I tried to find out what his concerns were and basically they boiled down to fear—fear of having sold at too low of a price, fear of not being able to find a new house, and fear of losing his 3.9 percent SBA loan. I immediately paged Mitch who was at church with his family. What happened next demonstrates how God covers us with His grace when we get sucker punched by the devil and have the breath of faith knocked out of us.

Mitch stepped outside the sanctuary to return my call. As he was dialing my number, and later while we were in conversation, two people walked by and immediately felt impressed to pray for him. They sensed that something was not right. Their gifts of discernment were certainly working at that point. I had the horrible responsibility to tell Mitch that the seller had rescinded his counter offer. His excuse for canceling the deal was that he did not receive our acceptance within the prescribed time period. Mitch intuitively knew that the Bible says, "We wrestle not against flesh and blood but against principalities, against powers, against the rulers of the darkness of this world, against spiritual wickedness in high places." We knew that this man was not our problem; however, he was allowing fear to manipulate him and our struggle transcended his reticence to sell.

I hung up the phone in a funk. To say that both of us were bluer than blue would be an understatement. I remember going through the rest of Sunday afternoon in a daze. We took the kids to a movie but I couldn't tell you what we saw because my emotions were raw. After two months of looking and finding the perfect house with one week to go, I was not prepared to have it ripped out from beneath us. We regrouped that evening on the phone and then I set up a meeting between the sellers, their agent, the Hargitays and myself.

To say that everyone was tense would be an understatement. I vaguely recall Mitch telling them how perfect they thought the house was for them. Being the salesperson that I am, I tried to isolate the sellers' objections. Ultimately, we isolated the three items mentioned previously: they wanted more money--$10,000 to be exact; they wanted more time to find a house—60 days; and they wanted assurance that they could move their $90,000 SBA loan to the property of their choice. I asked them that if we could deliver all three terms to them, would they sell the house to the Hargitays. I even went so far as to draw up a counter offer delineating those demands. However, they would not sign it that evening. Their position was to wait and see what the title insurance company would say about whether or not they could move the SBA loan to a new property. We left their guesthouse, somewhat encouraged, although we all realized that we still had a long way to go by Friday.

Monday dawned bright and early, and my first call was to the title insurance company to see if they would hold the SBA loan for 60 days while the seller searched for a new house to attach the loan to. Needless to say, this required more than just a sales representative's approval. Nevertheless, the early indications were positive that it could be accomplished. The title executives set about to creatively establish how they would make this work legally.

Meanwhile, I also received a call from Jorge, one of my investor clients who had just that day received a payoff on a loan that he had made on another piece of property. He was looking to reinvest and asked if I had anyone who needed a second mortgage. Oh baby, did I have someone! However, his only caveat was that he would have to charge at least 10 percent interest. I wasted no time in getting him over to see the house that we were negotiating to buy and to meet Mitch and Tracy. Being a member of our church as well, he considered what he did in the area of financing to be a ministry. The three of them hit if off immediately, and he proceeded to call the person who ran his trust to draw up the papers for the second loan.

I asked Mitch and Tracy if they wanted to look at other houses; however, both of them felt that this was their house. They were finished house hunting. They had found the one that they believed was for them and I agreed; not because I was tired of showing them houses, but because this house truly met all of their needs. Not only that, the Bible says that in the mouth of two or three witnesses a thing is confirmed, and we were all in agreement that this was their house. We just needed God to confirm the same thing to the seller. Monday passed without the husband giving his consent to sign the counter offer.

Even though we did not have a duly executed contract, we opened escrow as if we did because we needed the escrow officer to do things to expedite the closing on Friday. We ordered a termite report and inspected the house with the seller's knowledge and approval. Meanwhile, Garrett was working on getting the loan documents drawn up. Jorge, who was going to carry the second loan, was diligent in getting his papers in order for the Hargitays to sign. So everyone was acting as if we had a sale except the most important person, the seller.

By Tuesday, we had confirmation from the title company that they would not require the seller's SBA loan to be paid off. What they agreed to do was hold the loan in an escrow account until the seller had found a house and then they would secure the note with the new property. Moreover, they consented to give the seller 90 days in which to find a property and close on it. Even with this assurance, the seller still refused to sign the counter offer and officially sanction the sale of his house. We had given him everything that he wanted on Sunday night; however, he was reneging on his verbal agreement. Again, on Tuesday, I asked Mitch if they wanted to look at any other houses and the answer was still "No." During this time, the scripture the Lord had given me over a month ago came back to me about "the rebellious house." While I do not believe that the man was purposefully trying to break their hearts, he was still living in fear rather than facing his new future with a sense of faith and expectation. At least on Tuesday, this is what I perceived. I went to bed wondering how God was going to work all of this out.

Clap On—Clap Off

By Wednesday morning, it was make-it-or-break-it time. I had to go to Simi Valley on business, so I called Mitch and told him that as I was driving, I was going to do what our pastor, Jack Hayford, had been encouraging us to do for the past two-and-a-half months and that was to let "praise be our pathway." In other words, wherever we went we should go praising the Lord and see His presence brought into our situation. I didn't get out of Chatsworth. As I pulled out of our office's parking lot, I began to sing a song that I had written that had been featured on the Hosanna Integrity release *Men in Worship with Jack Hayford.* The song, "We Applaud Your Greatness," was written to encourage people to clap their hands in honor of the Lord with an understanding of the spiritual dynamism that can be released when they "clap their hands *and* shout unto God with a voice of triumph," according to Psalm 47:1. Until I read Harry and Cheryl Salem's book, *From Mourning to Morning,* Pastor Jack was the only person I had ever heard teach on the subject of the clapping of hands. Harry writes in their book:

> *Clapping is actually a form of spiritual warfare. When you clap your hands together, it is a sign of a guarantee that you believe, receive and walk in the promise God has given you for your miracle. You are clapping your hands together in agreement with God that the promise is given, received and fulfilled in Jesus' mighty name. Whether it is healing, provision of finances, restoration of your marriage or bringing a wayward child home, it is already a done deal.* (Or convincing a rebellious owner to sell his house. I just couldn't resist inserting that).
>
> *The devil does not want to turn you or your loved one loose or submit to your power, but he does not have any choice, as it says in this Scripture:*
>
> *"Through the greatness of Your power shall Your enemies submit themselves to You [with feigned and reluctant*

obedience]" (Psalm 66:3 AMP).

We needed submission now, so driving up Variel Avenue, I
began to sing:

> *I will not give that which costs me nothing,*
> *So when I clap my hands in honor of the Lord*
> *I lift my voice in praise and adoration:*
> *Together they become an instrument of war.*
>
>> *We applaud Your greatness; we applaud Your might;*
>> *And we shout to God in triumph, as we set ourselves to*
>> *fight*
>> *Every demon trembles when he hears our voices raised*
>> *Joined with loud applause affirming You are worthy to*
>> *be praised.*
>
> *I clap my hands to show I'm in agreement*
> *With what the Word of God says concerning me*
> *You're King of kings and Lord of lords forever*
> *With our applause we come to welcome royalty.*
>
>> *We applaud Your greatness; we applaud Your might;*
>> *And we shout to God in triumph, as we set ourselves to*
>> *fight*
>> *Every demon trembles when he hears our voices raised*
>> *Joined with loud applause affirming You are worthy to*
>> *be praised.*
>
> *Clap your hands make a joyful noise.*

By the time I got to this point in the song, I had turned left onto
Chatsworth Street and pulled over to the side of the road. I did this for
two reasons: First, in this part of the song, the singer is to respond by
clapping rhythmically to the beat; second, I didn't want to wreck my
car and have to believe God to heal me as well as change a seller's
fearful heart. So, I pulled over. However, the most compelling reason
for pulling over was that the power of the Holy Spirit was so strong
in my car that I had no choice. I continued singing:

> *Clap your hands make the darkness flee*

Clap your hands praise His majesty.

Now I was singing and clapping with such fervor that I knew something supernatural had taken over. My praises to God were elevated to a new level that I had not experienced before. As I sang the chorus, suddenly I saw in my mind a picture of the house that the Hargitays were attempting to buy. And just over the house was a funnel cloud—the kind that used to drive us to the basement when I lived in Missouri. Pictured there in the center of the funnel cloud were the sellers, both the husband and wife. As I continued singing and clapping, suddenly the cloud lifted above the house and with the sellers in tandem, blew off to the north, which was the direction that the sellers wanted to move.

In 1 Corinthians 12:9, the Apostle Paul writes about the gifts of the Spirit, and verse nine specifically mentions a supernatural impartation of faith. This is a different kind of faith than the one mentioned in Romans 10:17 that says, "So then faith *cometh* by hearing, and hearing by the word of God." Anyone can develop Romans 10:17 kind of faith by systematically putting the Word of God into your heart, by memorizing and meditating on the Word and confessing it out loud. The I Corinthians 12:9 kind of faith is a gift of the Spirit that is supernaturally given without having to do anything other than receive it when it is given. When I saw that funnel cloud lift off over the house and blow north toward Valencia, I knew that I knew that I knew that we had a deal. Supernatural faith had been imparted to me. God had definitely put his *Super* on my natural.

I turned my car around and drove straight back to the office and called Carlene, my escrow officer, and asked her to call the seller and tell him to come in to sign the contracts because we had a house to close on Friday. At this point, I was very careful to watch the words that came out of my mouth. I knew to do this by witnessing the actions of our church leaders when we were attempting to buy another church campus eight years prior to this transaction.

Church Growth

Purchasing the Van Nuys First Baptist Church was the fulfillment of a promise the Lord had given our pastor over fifteen years before.

However, during the escrow period a sticking point came up that forced our executive team to pull out of the deal. Suddenly, it looked like the deal was dead and that a builder was going to purchase the campus, tear down the church and build condominiums. During the ensuing twelve months, our leaders did not say one negative word about the experience. No one said, "Well I guess we didn't hear God," or "I guess God has something else for us." They said nothing because they believed God's original word to them—we were to purchase that campus.

Then, more than a year after pulling out of the deal, the leadership at Van Nuys First Baptist Church called and asked if our church still wanted to buy their property. It seems that the contractor couldn't build as many condos as he originally thought he could and wanted out. So, approximately 18 months from the time that we had originally started negotiations, we closed on the additional campus. Today, this eleven-acre campus houses not only the Church on the Way Sanctuary, but also the King's College and Seminary. I learned from observing our leaders that we need to watch what comes out of our mouth at all times. As it says in Romans 14:23b: "…for whatsoever *is* not of faith is sin." I purposed to watch my words in this situation and remain in faith too.

Cut to the Chase

When the escrow officer called me back and said that the seller was not going to sell the house to Mitch and Tracy, I didn't immediately question God or myself. Instead I called Mitch. However, he couldn't talk to me because he had a conversation going on his other line. I hung up not realizing that the seller was speaking directly to Mitch and Tracy at that very moment. A few minutes later my phone rang at the office and it was the seller. His words to me were, "If I do not sell my house to your buyers, it is going to break their hearts. I will sign the paperwork." With a hoop and a holler after hanging up, I immediately called Carlene and asked her to go to Valencia to sign the seller up after work at his place of business. She graciously agreed. Meanwhile, Mitch and Tracy went off to sign loan documents that Garrett had delivered.

I mentioned earlier that I play the organ at the Church on the

Way and, during this season, I was scheduled to play virtually every Wednesday night of the month. However, in His wisdom, God had seen into the future while the organ schedule was being made out the previous month and had prompted the music assistant to put another organist in the queue that night. Driving through the pouring rain to the business park that evening, I was in awe of what God was doing. Little did I know, He was not done yet.

Carlene and I were welcomed into the seller's office and were offered pizza. We gladly accepted. She started by having the sellers sign the escrow instructions and then quickly produced the grant deed. As the seller was signing his name to the deed that would transfer ownership over to Mitch and Tracy once recorded, he said, "I don't know why I am doing this." He repeated that again as I was showing him where to sign on the counter offer and other addenda to the purchase contract. Inwardly, I thought to myself, *I know why you are signing.* Outwardly, I just nodded my head and continued to point out the various places where he needed to sign to make this a legally binding contract. In thirty minutes time, we picked up our paperwork, thanked them profusely and left with a sigh of relief. The downpour of rain during the drive home was a sign to me of God's blessings being poured out on his children who trust Him.

Closing a Two-Day Escrow

With the biggest hurdle having been jumped over with the seller's signing the contract on Wednesday evening, Thursday should have been a day of funding the two loans and preparing for the recording of the deed on Friday morning. However, the lender for the first mortgage asked for a document before they would fund the loan and it so happened that Tracy's sister, who was their accountant, had that document at her house. So, no problem, we just run over to her house, get the paper and rush it back to the lender. Well, when there is a tent on your sister's house keeping poisonous gases inside to kill all of those pesky little termite critters, you do not just rush in, holding your nose, and grab the file. Fortunately, the tent was coming off that morning. Nevertheless, we couldn't get the lender the document in time to fund the loan on Thursday. Now we had to go to plan B.

At that time in Los Angeles County, the county recorder would allow you to do a special recording, provided you met certain guidelines. We now had no other options but to proceed with funding the loan on Friday morning and then have the title company stand in line at the county recorder's office to record the grant deed in the afternoon. This is how a special recording works.

The IRS rules stated that the buyer had to be living in the house no later than two years after the sale of the last principal residence. Therefore, Mitch and Tracy had spent much of Thursday packing and had the movers coming Friday morning. However, we could not allow them to start moving in until we had confirmation that the deed had recorded. At this point, everything having to do with getting the loan funded and recorded was out of my hands. I could only pray and be on call in case I needed to deliver a document anywhere at any time.

As Friday morning dawned, I asked the Lord to allow the wire from the lender to reach the title company early that morning so we would know that the funds were there and that the title officer would give the okay for the grant deed to be recorded. By 11:00 a.m., it would be possible to know if the wire had been received. Unfortunately, we had no word. I had to drive to downtown Los Angeles to talk to an executive at Bank of America about the foreclosures that I was marketing for her department, so I left without having received any news about the funding. Upon leaving the meeting somewhere between 1:30 and 2:00, I phoned Carlene to see if she had received any word. Everyone involved in this transaction knew that if the recording did not happen today before 5:00 p.m., there was no deal because the Hargitays would now owe the IRS $40,000 if we closed on Monday instead of Friday. Tensions mounted in my car.

Meanwhile, Mitch and Tracy had just about finished packing and were driving to the new house located in a beautiful area in the north part of the Valley. We had worked out a plan. Once I received word from Carlene or the title officer that we had confirmation that the deed was recorded, I would page Mitch and put in the numbers "1,1,1,1". This was our signal that the deal was done and they could start moving in.

I got back to the office around 2:30 and went right in to a meeting with the people who were buying a house that was tied up in knots. Oops, I am getting ahead of myself. You'll have to read about that story in the chapter on real estate contention. I did tell these buyers that I was going to have to take every phone call that came in during our meeting because of the urgency of the situation. They were very understanding. The phone only rang once or twice between 2:30 and 3:30. However, shortly after 3:30, I received a page over the loud speaker that I had a call on line one. Picking up the receiver, I heard Garrett's voice on the other end, and the words that I heard caused my heart to almost stop beating.

You Have Got to be Kidding!

"They've pulled the funds," was the first statement out of his mouth. Not, "Hello," not, "Hey, congratulations," but "They've pulled the funds," meaning that the lender found something wrong with the file and took their money back. At this late hour, it would be impossible to correct the problem, refund the loan and get it recorded. The county recorder's office closed in less than 90 minutes. After everyone's hard work, after the tears, after the prayers, after the faith that had been exercised, how could it end this way?

The next words out of Garrett's mouth almost made me want to climb through the phone line and choke him. "Gotcha!" He said. "It recorded a half hour ago. Here is the instrument recording number." I didn't have time to castigate him for almost giving this thirty-something REALTOR® a heart attack because I had to let Mitch and Tracy know the good news. They had movers parked across the street waiting for the signal to move in. I told him I was going to call them now and hung up.

Meanwhile, the Hargitays were parked in front of the house just waiting for that all-important "1,1,1,1" page. Evidently, Garrett had a faster phone than mine because his page reached Mitch first. When Mitch looked at the pager, he recognized Garrett's number.

"That's odd that Garrett would be paging me right now," Mitch said to Tracy. Trepidation tried to get a foothold so that fear could barge right on in. Instead, Mitch said, "I am not going to return his call just yet. I believe that Rodney is going to page me first." And no sooner had he said that than the "1,1,1,1" appeared on his LED display. A shout went up as Mitch and Tracy hugged each other and began to cry. Even their movers rejoiced with them. So, with less than an hour-and-a-half to go, they had officially bought a house. I stopped by the house that evening around 10 p.m., had a slice of pizza and rejoiced with them again over God's faithfulness in providing a home that met all of their needs—A Dream Home—if you will. We had a firsthand testimony like that of the Apostle Paul when he wrote in Philippians 4:13 that our "God will supply all your needs according to his riches in glory by Christ Jesus."

In case you are wondering about the sellers. They found a newer house in Valencia, moved into it and attached their SBA loan to the new property, thereby preserving that low 3.9 percent interest rate. Moreover, at one point during their negotiations to buy their house, the seller told me that he had gone to the new house early one morning and knelt down and prayed. God answered his prayers, too!

Jeremiah says to "Call unto me and I will answer you and show you great and mighty things which you do not know." We were in the midst of a miracle that began because we called unto the Lord. I do not mean to imply that we took this seller for a ride and conned him into doing something that he didn't want to do. On the contrary, he very much wanted to move to Valencia; however, fear was keeping him from taking the steps that would get him to where he really wanted to be. And his indecision was interfering with my buyers' need to close on a home by March 15.

It is obvious that God loves this man just as much as he loves Mitch and Tracy and has a plan of ultimate fulfillment for this seller's life. However, God is not moved by need. He is moved by faith. And the three of us were acting in faith, whereas the seller was not acting–period. Therefore, God honored our faith as we "called those things that be not as though they were."

I want to encourage you that no matter what kind of deadline you may be facing, God will come through if you trust Him and then act on what He shows you to do. As Jesus' brother James said, "Faith without works is dead." When that supernatural faith was imparted to me in my car, it was not because I was following some rote formula of clapping. You can't clap your way into a house. You get your dream house through listening to what the Spirit would speak to you and then acting on those instructions.

If I have intrigued you thus far with this rollar-coaster testimony of God's supernatural provision in obtaining a "dream" home, then let me guide you even further into this "real estate revelation" from the Scriptures and my own real-life stories. Continue with me as we delve deeper into discovering what we each need to do to enter and possess our own Promised Land.

CHAPTER 2

Extreme Makeover: The Earth Edition

In the beginning God created the heavens and the earth. The earth was without form, and void; and darkness was on the face of the deep. And the Spirit of God was hovering over the face of the waters.

(Genesis 1:1, 2)

I have to admit up front, I was dragged kicking and screaming into the real estate sales field. I did *not* want to be here. Nor did I think I would still be selling real estate eighteen years later. Hollywood had phoned and I had taken the call. For almost three years during the mid 1980's, I worked for ABC Entertainment.

My last two seasons with the network were spent reading scripts for the Prime Time Programming Department and writing synopses about the nighttime dramas, movies for television and miniseries that the network was airing. These were sent out to the ABC affiliates to let them know in advance what kind of dreck, I mean, dramas we were putting on the air. While the episodic scripts were formulaic, predictable and not that much fun to read, I did get out of my cubicle from time to time to go with the program executives to the studio's production lots and watch rough cut screenings of some of the shows.

One time, when *Dynasty* and its spin-off *The Colbys* were on the air, I caught a tracking error between the two shows that had characters crossing over on the wrong airdates. My boss at ABC was gracious enough to give me the credit for spotting the error and saving the network and production company embarrassment. In return, I got a bottle of scotch from the producers, which I promptly gave to one of the exec's secretaries. Oh, life in Hollywood! I believed that I would be famous like the meaning of my name, Rodney. But hey, I am getting ahead of myself. I will discuss meanings of names and the importance of our words in the chapter *Names...and a Dog Called Bon Queesha.*

My Very First Dream Home

Before I started work at ABC in October of 1983, I had my first dream about real estate sometime earlier in the year shortly after I was married in December of 1982. I still remember that dream vividly 21 years later. Just like seventy-five-year-old Abram received a promise from God that he would possess a land, I am in the process of possessing the land God showed me in 1983.

When I awoke the morning after my dream, I described to Valerie about seeing a house built into the side of the hill. I only saw the house from the back, and it appeared to have two long levels running parallel to each other. On the left side of the property was another wing, forming an L shape to the house--at least that's the way it looked from my vantage point in the dream. Because the residence was built on the side of a hill, its back yard was not flat. Ivy coming down from the back side covered the sloping lot. I remember telling Valerie that we would own this house someday. That was a pretty bold statement for a person who was barely making minimum wage at the time of the dream. Had I known then that what I saw in my dream was a real house and where that house was located, I am not sure I would have had the faith to make that statement.

Fast forwarding to my tenure at ABC, sometime during the first year-and-a-half of working there, I was rear-ended on my way to the office. Chiropractic appointments were set and I began the healing process. On a typical day, I would leave my Century City office and drive north on Beverly Glen to world famous Sunset Boulevard where I would turn right and then make an immediate left back onto Beverly Glen to go home to North Hollywood. On this particular day, I was daydreaming and not paying much attention to where I was going until I got almost to Sunset. It was then that I remembered my chiropractic appointment and that I needed to turn *left* on Sunset Boulevard and not right so that I could catch the San Diego Freeway to the Valley. As I whipped over to the left hand turn lane at Sunset, I distinctly heard the Holy Spirit speak to me, "I am going to show you your house."

For those who do not know their Los Angeles geography, I was in Beverly Hills and about to cross over to Bel-Air. Those two cities make up two-thirds of what is referred to as the "Platinum Triangle," home to some of the most expensive real estate in the world. Holmby Hills, location of Aaron Spelling's 50,000 square foot mansion, rounds out the other third of the Platinum Triangle.

As I tooled along Sunset, I passed a certain well-known street in Bel-Air. Again I heard the voice of the Spirit who said, "Third house on the left." Since I needed to be at my chiropractor's office in Northridge, I didn't have time to turn and investigate. So, on the following Saturday, I drove back over the hill to Sunset Boulevard to the street where the Spirit had spoken to my spirit, "Third house on the left." Driving slowly and deliberately I reached the third driveway, which led up a hill and around to the front of the house. Going past the driveway, I saw a long two-story house from the back that was built into the side of a hill with another building and/or wing off to the left making what appeared to be an L shape. The two stories were long and parallel to each other like what I saw in my dream. Because the house was built into a hill, it had a sloping yard—and you guessed it—covered with ivy.

Another bonus, which I didn't see in my dream, was a tennis court at the bottom of the lot. However, the thing that impacted me most was the gate. Above the entrance written on the arch were written words in another language which mean "House of Contentment" or "Happy Home." Needless to say I was thrilled. For a twenty-five-year-old renter to literally find his "Promised Land" in this manner was awesome. I can hear the wheels in your mind turning, *When and how did you buy this piece of prime real estate?* As of this writing, I have yet to purchase that particular house. I have researched title on it and checked on it from time to time, yet I have not been prompted to do anything else other than wait on God's timing. That was a lesson Abram had to learn as well. Had he waited for God, the situation in the Middle East might be a lot more peaceful than at present.

If you do not know what I am talking about, let's look at Genesis 15. In verse 4, God promises Abram that the heir to his fortune will not be a servant in his house but a child from his own body. Abram believed Him and verse six says that it was credited to him as righteousness. Furthermore, God goes on to tell Abram that he is going to possess the land that he was promised. Wanting to know *how* he would possess it, he questioned God. At this point in the story, God told Abram to bring him a heifer, goat, ram, dove and a pigeon. The heifer, goat, and ram were cut in half and laid side by side. When Abram fell into a deep sleep, the Lord walked between those sacrificed animals and, in essence, cut covenant with Abram.

Contracts are NOT Made to be Broken

We do not understand a covenant very well in today's litigious society. We've all heard it said that contracts were made to be broken. Most real estate contracts have contingencies that let the buyer opt out without losing his or her deposit if certain conditions are not met. However, a covenant is much stronger and more binding than a contract. In fact, a covenant can only be broken through death. When two people made a covenant in Abram's day, they exchanged strengths and weaknesses with each other. For instance, let's say that a family of mechanical engineers and carpenters were to cut covenant with the Johnson family. They would get my ability to recognize good real estate investments and musical gifts. In return, our family would benefit from their engineering experience, of which I have none. They would take my strengths as well as my weaknesses. My ability to "hammer like lightning"—meaning that I never strike twice in the same place—would now be covered by someone who had those skills that I lack.

Abram had a covenant with Elohim, the God of Creation. Abram's weaknesses were replaced by God's strengths. Even though it appeared that he might be too old to father a child, he waited in faith. For awhile, this appeared to have satisfied him until his wife Sarai came up with an idea to help Elohim along in producing a child. Since she hadn't been able to conceive, she had the not-so-bright idea of letting Abram have sex with her Egyptian maid, Hagar. Without consulting God regarding his covenant, Abram consented and produced a son, Ishmael, through Hagar. As a result of this union, the Arab nations were birthed. And, like many families today who can't seem to get along, they have been at war with the nation birthed through Abram and Sarai ever since. That nation is Israel.

Abram learned a very difficult lesson about timing. In real estate, timing is a critical component as well. Up to this point, my wife and I have not felt that Bel-Air is where we want to raise our children. Although, I have not let the price of real estate in Bel-Air deter me from my dream.

I think a lot about what bestselling business author, Robert Kiyosaki, said in his book, *Rich Dad Poor Dad*, about the difference between his two dads. When presented with a real estate investment opportunity, *Poor Dad,* his biological father, used to say, "I could never afford that." While *Rich Dad,* his business mentor, used to tell him, "Never say *'I can't afford it.'* Instead ask, *'How can I afford it?'*"

By asking a question, we keep our minds open to possibilities that God might pour into us. Had Abram questioned how he was to produce this promised child from his own body, he could have had an eye-opening conversation with Elohim, the God of creation. Like *Poor Dad* who thought he couldn't afford real estate, Abram thought Sarai was not able to conceive.

Contrary to what most people believe, you do not need lots of money to be a real estate investor. I purchased my first house with no money down, and the three houses that I have owned up to this point have all had some form of seller financing structured into the original deal. Even though Sarai had gone through menopause, there was still a baby to be birthed through her body.

Many times we short change what God would do in and through us because of our mindset. *Rich Dad* passed on many other lessons with spiritual truths as well, particularly about the way we think. I would encourage those readers wanting to increase their knowledge of building wealth to check out the whole library of *Rich Dad* books.

You can find them on my website at www.RodneyJohnson.com.

After dreaming of a house and then finding it, my faith has grown to the point that I believe God truly has a promised land for each and every child of His. It does not have to be a multi-million dollar property in the Platinum Triangle or Canaan land, for that matter. It's a place for each one of us to call our own, to rule and reign in this life and to exercise dominion. When I actually did buy my first house five years later, God again spoke to me in the same manner he spoke to Abram when He said, "Get out of your country, from your family and from your father's house, to a land that I will show you." My direction was to give my 30-day notice to my landlord before I had actually bought a house. I will go into detail about what happened in the chapter entitled *Trust - Fear = A Great Way to Live.* Learning to trust like Abram ultimately did is not always easy, although it is infinitely more exciting and fulfilling when we learn to live in faith as he did.

Abram, who became Abraham The Father of The Faith, is going to be weaving in and out through many of the chapters in this book. However, let's go back to the beginning and look at the first father, Adam. God talks about real estate in the first verse of the Bible.

In the beginning, God created the heavens and the earth.

And the second verse recounts the first remodel.

And the earth was without form and void; and darkness was over the face of the deep. And the Spirit of God moved upon the face of the waters.

If I was still working at ABC, and we were going to do a Movie for Television about Genesis 1:2, I would title it: *Extreme Makeover, The Earth Edition.* In between those two verses in Genesis chapter one, thousands of years have elapsed. God did not create something chaotic. Something cataclysmic happened between *God created* and *the earth was without form and void,* which caused God to literally do an extreme makeover. For a more detailed study of this scripture, I refer the reader to Billye Brim's book, *The Blood and the Glory,*

34

which can also be purchased at my website, www.RodneyJohnson.com. Because God redeems, He *moved upon the face of the waters* and began recreating this ball of dirt and water we call earth. Additionally, when He created mankind, He gave responsibilities to them to assist in this remodel, as outlined in Genesis 1:28.

> And God blessed them, and God said unto them, "Be fruitful, and multiply, and replenish the earth, and subdue it: and have dominion over the fish of the sea, and over the fowl of the air, and over every living thing that moveth upon the earth."

No matter what your economic situation is right now, I believe God has a place for you to call your own. If you do not desire to actually own real estate, you can still be a source of light in the apartment or house that you rent. You are not relieved of your duties to replenish the earth and subdue it.

Answer the Call

In September of 2003, our congregation at The Church on the Way, Van Nuys, California, was called to a three-day fast by our then Senior Pastor, Scott Bauer. Only days before the fast began, the Lord spoke to Scott and said, *"You have no idea how important this fast is."* None of us knew then that less than a month later, Scott would be called home to his heavenly reward when an aneurysm burst in his brain, taking his life at age 49. In preparation for the fast, I asked the Lord if there was something that He wanted to speak to me and He gave me the following word, which was shared with our congregation at the conclusion of the three-day fast:

> The Lord would say, *"I have given you spiritual real estate. Your faith is the title deed to this property. Do not fear that you will have to take a loan to receive this spiritual real estate, because the price has been paid in full through the blood of Jesus Christ. The Holy Spirit is the deposit, or the promissory note, until the redemption of the purchased*

possession. Your adversary has sought to take your territory through adverse possession. However, that can only be legally accomplished if the true owner does nothing. Therefore, enforce the legality of your title deed through the words of your mouth. Come into agreement with My Word and speak it aloud. And thus serve notice on the devil that he is being evicted—because you are the legal owner of this territory."

For definitions of real estate terms like "adverse possession" and others, see the *Glossary of Real Estate Terms* at the end of the book. Maybe you are wondering what "spiritual real estate" is. In the chapter, *How To Get Everything You Want,* I will relate a story of how author John Dawson prayed through his neighborhood and literally saw it changed over the years into a peaceful place populated with people who loved God. He was enforcing the title deed to his spiritual real estate through prayers for his neighbors. This word became one of the focal points of our fast, and I believe that it can be an encouragement to you too as you seek God for what He would have you rule and reign over in this life. As I Corinthians 14:3 states "…he who prophesies speaks edification and exhortation and comfort to men." May you be encouraged to seek out and believe God for the real estate He has for you, both spiritual and physical.

Perhaps some of you are thinking, "Rodney, you are scaring me with this talk about God speaking to you and giving you prophetic words, especially about real estate. Those kinds of things quit happening after the Bible was given. We do not have a need for prophecy because we have God's word. Furthermore, does it not say that 'we know in part and we prophesy in part and when that which is perfect is come, then those things will be done away with?' Is not the Bible the perfect thing that Paul was referring to when he wrote that?"

If you have never been exposed to prophetic words, then those questions might be running through your mind. There are some theologians who teach that the gifts of the Holy Spirit have ceased or been dispensed with when the canon of scripture was finalized. People who believe this way are called dispensationalists. I have some very dear friends who sit under dispensationalist teachers.

Instead of arguing theology, what I want to do is encourage everyone to get into the Word of God and see what He would speak directly to you regarding real estate and other important aspects of your life.

In John 1:1, Jesus is referred to as the Word. The Greek translation of "the Word" is logos, which means *the said word.* All of scripture can be referred to as the logos or *said Word of God. Rhema* is another Greek term that is also translated as *word.* Rhema is distinguished from logos as *the saying word of God.* In the prophetic word related above, the Holy Spirit ignited certain scriptures to give me the gist of the prophecy. This is an example of scripture becoming a rhema word. In fact, sometimes the Holy Spirit will take a scripture that almost jumps off the pages of the Bible and it will speak directly to whatever you are facing at the time. This is an example of a *logos* word becoming a *rhema* word to you.

When the Lord spoke to me through my scripture reading in Ezekiel about the "rebellious house," He was giving me a rhema word regarding how to approach the purchase for Mitch and Tracy. If rhema words are new to you, do not despair. God is speaking to you too, and not just to preachers and people who write books. The overall context of I Corinthians 13 is that everything should be done in love. So to my dispensationalist friends, I say, *I love you and pray God's best for you. Do not put down the book, yet. As you believe in the sovereignty of God, may you come to know and experience that He has sovereignly declared that you are to rule and reign with Him in this life. May you rule and reign over the real estate that He has for you, and may you actively participate with Him in seeing it become a blessing to you and to all of your sphere of influence.*

It is not my intent to make a jab at those who believe differently than I do. Instead, through the exciting examples I describe in this book, I hope that everyone will see that God has never rescinded his commandment to replenish the earth and to have dominion. David records in Psalm 8:6 "You have made him to have **dominion** over the works of Your hands; You have put all things under his feet...." In order to do that, it will require us using all of the gifts He has enumerated in His Word.

Like Abram who received the command to get out of his father's house and into the land that the Lord would show him, you will need faith to possess your land. You'll need the right mindset to possess your land. You'll need obedience to possess your land. And you'll need God's timing to possess your land. You can and will possess your land if you make a commitment to God's word and do what it says to do. You'll learn to hear the voice of the Good Shepherd and when He, through the Holy Spirit, says, "Third house on the left" you'll know that is from Him.

Having worked in real estate sales for nearly twenty years, I like to think of God as the broker—the One who is ultimately responsible—who employs us as His agents to do the work of subduing the earth and having dominion over the work of His hands. This helps me in my thinking to remember who truly is "in charge" regarding any real estate deal I might be involved with.

Now, since I happen to practice my real estate trade in the Los Angeles area, people often ask me about various well-known areas in this city. Therefore, if you have ever wondered about Beverly Hills and other renowned neighborhoods, I invite you to continue with me into the next chapter and get The 411 on 90210 and Other Famous Zip Codes...

CHAPTER 3

The 411 on 90210 and Other Famous Zip Codes

So why is real estate really necessary? Wouldn't it be simpler to just rent a house or apartment somewhere and let someone else take care of the responsibilities of the upkeep? I suppose that is some people's mindset; however, I do not believe that is God's heart in the matter. The first three chapters in the book of Genesis are all about the very first real estate transaction. And from the look of things, it appears that God places a high priority on His property. In essence, He's leased the earth to us and told us to develop it. And like every lease, there is a start date and an end date. If you are a student of biblical prophecy, maybe you are thinking this lease is about to run out and we shouldn't be concerned with things as "worldly" as real estate. I would like to challenge that thinking. Have you ever heard the phrase "occupy until He comes?" Let's live like Jesus is coming back today and work and plan as if He is coming back a hundred years from now. One synonym for the word "occupy" is "possess." So let's continue possessing our promised land.

We've already seen that God intended for us to rule and reign with him. What you may not realize is that what happens in the earthly realm is a pattern of what is going on in the heavenlies. In the Lord's Prayer, Jesus taught His disciples to pray "…Thy will be done on earth as it is in heaven."

From all of the explicit and careful directions God gave surrounding the building of his temple, it's obvious He wanted it to be beautiful to reflect His glory. In fact, my pastor said this last

Sunday that if Solomon's temple were built today, the cost would be $5 Billion. That's a "B" folks—not five million. So before you start criticizing some contemporary ministry for building a beautiful building, remember that the first temple was lavish beyond comparison.

When Solomon's temple was completed, the Bible records that the glory of God filled the temple like a cloud. I believe that our homes should also reflect His beauty and glory. Last summer, we took four months and completely re-landscaped our yard—front and back. Today, I look out and see French doors leading to a serene courtyard with a brick seating area and a three-tiered water fountain. An outdoor fireplace by the replastered and retiled pool adds warmth and ambiance. I thrill to see the vibrant colors of the snap dragons and roses in bloom. In short, I sense God's presence because of the beauty of nature in our yard. However, that beauty would not have the symmetry and order without Kolleen's plans, Johnny's implementation of those plans and a systematic watering and weeding schedule to keep it looking beautiful. You do not have to have a three-tiered fountain in your yard to reflect God's glory. You were uniquely created by your Creator and the creativity He's placed within you can shine through.

I take great pleasure in knowing that this September a young couple from our church will be using our backyard for their wedding reception. Your home can reflect God's glory, too. If you have yet to purchase a house, begin to treat the apartment or house you are renting as if it were your own. This could be key in the process of you obtaining your first property. In the parable of the talents in Matthew 25:14-30, the man who doubled his talents was also given the one talent from the man who was fearful and hid his talent. The steward exhorted him that he who is faithful in little is faithful also in much. If you will begin to be faithful with the property right where you are—even if you do not own it—you will show yourself as someone who can be entrusted with more responsibilities.

We also allow the City of Los Angeles to use our house as a polling place in most of the elections we've had since the 2000 presidential race. We do not do this to curry political favor. Instead, we see it as an opportunity to bless our neighbors. Before the polls open, we've prayed God's protection and blessing on those who will step onto our property throughout the day. If we were not homeowners, we would not have this privilege.

In the United States, our government also recognizes that homeownership is a good thing and rewards those who purchase and maintain properties. For instance, if Mitch and Tracy from Chapter One were to sell their house today, they could claim a gain of $500,000 tax-free! Moreover, they wouldn't have to buy again within two years like they had to do back in 1996. (I currently have clients whose plan is to buy a house every two years, live in it, improve it and then sell it for a profit and take the tax free gain from their principle residence). For more information on the tax benefits of owning real estate, visit my website at www.RodneyJohnson.com and order *The Insider's Guide to Real Estate Investing Loopholes* by Diane Kennedy and Dolf De Roos.

If Mitch and Tracy owned a rental property, the government would allow them to depreciate the cost of the building and deduct that depreciation on their taxes as if it were a loss, even though in reality the property probably went up in value in the last year. These are legal tax loopholes that our government encourages everyone to take advantage of. And if you really want to be a blessing to your city, the government also makes grants and attractive loans available to landlords who will buy properties in socio-economically depressed areas, fix them up and rent them out at reasonable rates. Real estate is one vehicle through which you can be a blessing to countless people. Abraham was one of the richest men in the Bible. Like him, you can be blessed so that you can, in turn, be a blessing to others.

Another reason I like real estate so much is that it spurs creativity. When we bought our first "fixer-upper" house, we had countless outlets for our creativity by designing a new kitchen, choosing plants for the front yard, deciding on a color palette for the whole house, and coming up with a marketing campaign when it was time to sell. I get so much satisfaction driving by that first house and seeing that it continues to be one of the best houses on the street instead of one of the worst—like it was when we first bought it.

People who live in countries that allow private citizens to own real estate will generally have more desire and motivation to better themselves than those living in countries where the government owns all of the land. Immigrants come to the United States every day with dreams of making a better life, including owning their own home. In fact, I have one client who is a single woman from a European country who now owns 23 houses in Los Angeles County—give or take a house or two.

Because she has been allowed to own property, she is also in a position to be a blessing to others. I have observed her generosity first-hand when she bought her neighbor's house last summer and paid them 20 percent more than the property appraised for. To the credit of the homeowners, they were also believers who had made their house a place for God's glory to dwell. In this case, it was a win/win for both parties because the buyer got a house with the "feeling" she wanted and the sellers were rewarded for years of faithfulness to their God and church.

From a practical standpoint, another reason why you should be considering real estate is that it provides asset protection when the stock market is in decline. If you have as part of your plan to buy and hold real estate for the long term, historically, it will appreciate significantly. Even in a real estate downturn, you can make money. In fact, during the 1990's when prices dropped dramatically in Los Angeles, my income almost doubled in 1994 when I began to sell foreclosures. However, had I really been trying to get financially free, I would have bought one house a year from 1990-1999 for $200,000 or less. Today, those ten houses would be worth $500,000 or more each. If I had put 10 percent down on each one and taken out a loan of $180,000, I would owe less than $1,800,000 on properties worth $5,000,000 today. Moreover, my tenants would be paying the mortgage for me while I reaped the benefit of appreciation.

I have learned not to beat myself up for neglecting to purchase those rentals in the past decade. Instead, I am of the opinion that more good deals are coming my way and that I am going to take advantage of them, as I hope you will. If the last part about having mortgages of $1,800,000 scares you, or you think it is unbiblical, I urge you to keep reading, particularly the chapter entitled *Owing No Man Anything?* However, for now, we need to examine how you find those "counsellors" who will ensure your real estate "safety."

CHAPTER 4

"Rah, Rah, Sis Boom Bah, Go Team!"

Now it came to pass in those days that He went out to the mountain to pray, and continued all night in prayer to God. And when it was day, He called His disciples to Himself; and from them He chose twelve whom He also named apostles: Simon, whom He also named Peter, and Andrew his brother; James and John; Philip and Bartholomew; Matthew and Thomas; James the son of Alphaeus, and Simon called the Zealot; Judas the son of James, and Judas Iscariot who also became a traitor.

(Luke 6:12-16)

After having killed his brother Abel, Cain was confronted by God and asked where his brother was. He responded, "Am I my brother's keeper?" And so, almost from the beginning, man has tried to go it alone. Even before that, Cain's father, Adam, blamed his wife, Eve, for giving him the fruit from the tree of the knowledge of good and evil, which they were forbidden to eat. Again, the tendency was to go it alone. However, Jesus Christ was referred to as the Last Adam and he did just the opposite of the first Adam. He built a team of twelve men whom he trained for three years during his earthly ministry who were able to take his message to the entire world. It is interesting to note that Matthew was a tax collector. The

Master obviously needed someone on his team who had knowledge of finances and the law, which may have been one of the reasons Matthew was chosen to be in the inner circle of twelve.

Like most successful endeavors, real estate requires having a strong team around you. One of your first steps to getting started in real estate is to build a team. Do not try to do it alone. Proverbs 11:14 tells us that in the multitude of counselors there is safety. If we have trusted individuals around us with more knowledge in certain areas than we have, we can be kept from making mistakes—provided we heed their wise counsel.

Put Me in, Coach

My three kids all excel in their respective sports of baseball, volleyball and soccer. When they were starting out, the coach was usually a parent or other relative who volunteered. As they progressed in their abilities and were asked to join more competitive teams, the level of coaching went up, as did the caliber of the other team members. For my two oldest children, one of whom is playing college baseball and the other who is being recruited by college scouts to play volleyball, they are building their own team. They both have a personal trainer, a chiropractor, a podiatrist, and orthopedic doctors to help them with specific treatments and skills development. My son also has a pitching coach. My volleyball player seeks individual instruction from her coach from time-to-time as she learns a new position. Even my thirteen-year-old soccer player has a personal trainer. Recently, my volleyball star tried out for the Junior National team and was competing against girls who were four to five inches taller than her. Yet, the competition only spurred her on to try harder. At the end of the grueling three-hour try out, she was one of 24 girls out of over 300 asked to scrimmage on a court with the top players. The team surrounding her caused her to lift her own level of play. The same thing happened with my daughter who plays soccer. For the last two seasons, she has been invited to participate on the Southern California Olympic Development Program (ODP). I have never seen her work harder. So what am I saying? The better your team members are, the better you will be.

Who's on First? What's on Second?

If you are building a volleyball team, you need specific players like a good setter, a tall middle blocker, an outside hitter with great jumping ability, an opposite hitter, and defensive specialists who can dig the kills from the other team before they hit the floor. Each position has a specific skills set. In your real estate team, the following "players" should also be a part of your team: a REALTOR®, mortgage broker, accountant, attorney, escrow officer, title officer, home inspector, home warranty representative, geologist, and surveyor to name the most common. You will not use every one of these team members on every transaction; however, if you are buying a hillside property, you are going to want a geologist to check for soil stability before paying hundreds of thousands of dollars for that room with a view.

REALTOR® is a Two Syllable Word

Let's begin with a word I know best and the one you'll probably use most often—a REALTOR®. By the way, when pronouncing this word, say "Real-Tor," not "Real-a-tor." It is a two syllable word, not three. You'll be surprised at the number of people who mispronounce it, including other REALTORS®.

A REALTOR® is a member of the National Association of REALTORS®, which upholds a code of ethics. Not every person who has a broker's or agent's license is a REALTOR®. So, as you begin to build your team, ask your prospective real estate agent if he or she is a member of the National Association of REALTORS®. However, an affirmative answer to this question does not automatically mean they are the right one for you.

Let's look at some of the things a REALTOR® can and should do for you. If you are looking to purchase real estate, a good REALTOR® should ask you some specific questions about the kind of properties you are looking for. Do not be put off by these questions. At this stage of the process, you are deciding if you want to work with a particular agent and vice versa. Your questions to the agent and their questions of you will help both of you decide if there is a match regarding working together.

There are basically two kinds of agents: an agent who represents buyers and one who represents sellers. They are known as Buyer's Agents and Listing Agents, respectively. Most agents will fulfill either of these roles throughout the course of a year. Sometimes they will represent Buyers and other times Sellers. Occasionally, they will represent both parties in a transaction. In this case, they are known as a Dual Agent. By law, a Broker can represent both parties to a transaction if it is fully disclosed and both parties agree to it. For instance, if you call a listing agent and ask him to show you the property, you could end up being represented by a person who has a written contract with the seller. It's not necessarily a bad thing; however, it's not always in your best interest either. For the purposes of finding and purchasing real estate, it's usually better to find a Buyer's Agent who will work on your behalf and negotiate the best price and terms. If that agent is aggressive, he or she may come up with a listing of their own that fits your needs. In that instance, you decide whether you want a dual agency. When this happens in my business, I tell my sellers and buyers that I know they will have a good agent on both sides of the table, Me!

One way to find a good REALTOR® is to ask other successful investors who they use. You should ask the referring party what their experience was like working with the agent. Have they used her more than once? Would they use her again? What is her area of expertise? If you do not know any successful investors, consider joining a real estate investment club in your city. Most major cities will have one or more of these clubs, and they can be a great source for finding other members of your team.

Once you have a candidate or two to interview, call each REALTOR® and ask for an appointment. I suggest meeting them in person so that you can gauge their people skills. After all, the REALTOR® you select will be representing you and your offer to the seller of the house you want to purchase. Here is a beginning list of questions to ask your potential Buyer's Agent:

1. *How long have you been in business?* You do not necessarily have to have someone who's been in business for 30 years. A brand new agent can be great because they

will aggressively find you properties in order to secure your business.

2. *What areas do you serve?*

3. *What do you like best about your job?*

4. *What do you like least about your job?*

5. *What services do you offer for a new investor?*

6. *What are the hours I can call you?*

7. *Do you have free website services where I can search for the houses myself?*

8. *What has been your experience in helping buyers with creative financing needs?*

9. *Are you willing to make your commission a part of the financing?* The answer does not have to be yes; however, if they are willing to do that, it may allow you to buy a property you couldn't otherwise purchase.

10. *How many houses or investment properties do you own?*

11. *What are your personal goals for real estate investments?* Listen carefully to this answer. If they are not planning on investing in real estate, ask why. This question could be one of the keys to deciding whether or not you want to work with them because an agent with no plan to own real estate is obviously just a sales person.

(To download a comprehensive list of questions to ask a potential REALTOR®, visit www.RodneyJohnson.com and click on "Free Reports." We have questions to ask a Buyer's Agent and a different set for a Seller's Agent.)

I find that some buyers are very cavalier about whom they choose to work with. Like a bee sucking nectar from a flower, they take what they can get from one agent and then move on to the next, not realizing that they are in danger of cross pollination. By cross pollination I mean that, like a bee that will take the sweet stuff out of a flower without noticing it has pollen on its feet and will pollinate the next flower it lands on, a buyer can end up muddying the water without even realizing it.

What happens is this: one agent may show you a house and the next agent you "land on" may have access to the same Multiple Listing Service (MLS) information and want to show you the same house. Then it becomes a question of ethics for you about which agent really brought you the property first and deserves the opportunity to work with you. To avoid this situation, I would very carefully select an agent to work with in the area where you want to purchase and then remain loyal to them.

Another way to find an agent who would be a good match for you is to visit open houses and talk to them about the area. Find out how much they know about issues affecting the community. Stay away from a broker from out of the area where you want to purchase. Why? Because other than their one listing, they probably won't list anything else in the area and they do not really have a handle on what it's like to live in that particular community.

Once you have selected an agent to work with, they will probably want to connect you with a good mortgage broker. (For those who take issue with Christians going into debt, please see *Owing No Man Anything?* in the next chapter). A mortgage broker is someone who also has a real estate license in his particular state. Instead of finding houses, he will find you a good mortgage. He will have access to literally hundreds of programs. Once he has taken your loan application, it's his job to start shopping investors to find you the program that best fits your needs.

Maybe you are thinking, "Why don't I just go to my bank?" You could. It is possible that your bank will have a good loan program for which you qualify. If you feel comfortable doing this then, by all means, go ahead. You will not necessarily be charged more fees for going to a mortgage broker, though. Their investors pay them to do the processing of the loan so that you can get as good or better rates than you could from a bank or savings and loan. Please know that I am not pushing a mortgage broker over another lending institution. I think it is important to have relationships with a mortgage broker and a banker. Every time my bank changes Vice Presidents, I immediately go and introduce myself to the new person. I want that executive on my team as well. For instance, if I have the opportunity to bid on a house up for auction, I want to be able to withdraw my money and put it back in the bank without penalty. Knowing the Vice President can be helpful in those situations. He or she can also be a good source for alerting you to potential houses the bank might be taking back due to a default.

Maybe some of you are thinking, "I have really bad credit and doubt that I could qualify for a conventional mortgage." Others who are self-employed may be concerned that the expenses they have from their business will lower their income to a point where they can't qualify. Do not let fear keep you from pursuing your dream. I didn't have to qualify for a loan for either of the first two houses that I bought. "How did you do that?" you might ask. In both cases, the seller carried the loan for us. For our first house, we didn't even have to come up with a down payment. In the third house we bought, the seller carried a second loan and deferred payments for one year. So I hope you are beginning to see that there is more than one way to buy a house.

You Get What You Pay For

If you are starting to recognize that God wants you to rule and reign in the area of real estate, I hope you will not bypass this next person on your team. You are going to need a great accountant as you begin to accumulate properties. If you choose the right one, you can end up paying little or no taxes legally. Certified Public Accountant, Diane Kennedy, author of *The Insider's Guide to Real Estate Investing Loopholes*, says in her May 3, 2005 eNewsletter:

> *If you or your spouse can qualify as a real estate professional and you are currently paying taxes, then one of two things is wrong:*
>
> *(1) You do not own enough real estate, OR*
>
> *(2) Your advisor hasn't used the real estate loopholes available for you.*

I changed accountants when I incorporated. At our last meeting, I learned that we had saved $11,000 in self-employment tax by keeping accurate records and documenting our expenses. A good accountant can and should save you thousands of dollars more than they cost. I cringe when I am talking to potential sellers and hear them say that they do not have an accountant because they don't want to spend the money. Do not be "penny wise and pound foolish." Your tax planning should be done well in advance—particularly not the week before April 15.

A good accountant will advise you about the three types of income: earned income, portfolio income, and passive income, and how each kind is taxed. If you are working at a job, you are making earned income and have very few tax breaks. Furthermore, if you do not work, you do not get paid. Portfolio income is money that comes in from savings accounts, stocks, bonds, and mutual funds. You do not have to work for this income other than to accumulate the funds at some point in order to generate the income from your portfolio. Passive income, which has the greatest tax benefits in most cases, comes from rents collected on properties owned, interest earned from loans you have made, and royalties from intellectual property.

Your accountant should also advise you about ways to legally avoid paying taxes with your real estate. Three of the most common ways to do this are through exchanges, refinances, and selling your primary residence every two years. If you have an investment property, and have depreciated it to the point where it does not make sense to keep it any more, a 1031 exchange can defer capital gains indefinitely. Your REALTOR® should be knowledgeable about how to set this up, and your accountant should be advising you when it is time to sell and buy another property of equal or greater value. Your accountant should also be advising you on the benefits of refinancing and pulling cash out. Hopefully, this is part of a plan to acquire more real estate, while retaining your other investment property. Some homeowners like to sell their primary residence every two years, as is currently allowed by the IRS, and take a tax-free capital gain up to $500,000 for a married couple or $250,000 for a single person.

To find a good accountant who is knowledgeable about real estate, ask other rich people who own more than one property for their recommendation. Your REALTOR® should be a source for you to consult, as well. Do not ask your poor relative for tax advice. I am not belittling your poor relative, just being pragmatic about protecting the wealth that you will begin to accumulate as you start acquiring properties. I repeat: do not skip this important member of your team.

Heard Any Good Attorney Jokes Recently?

I have heard more than one broker say that some attorneys get their broker's license so that they can screw up their own deals. While attorneys have been the butt of many jokes, they do provide a significant service for the real estate industry. Some states use attorneys as a matter of course in all of their closings. Other states may rely on escrow officers; however, issues will come up from time-to-time when the legal advice of an attorney is warranted. In California, where I do most of my real estate business, attorneys are not part of the every day course of an escrow.

There have been issues arise in multi-million dollar transactions where I have strongly encouraged my client to retain the services of an attorney to protect their interests from unscrupulous sellers. Many cities will have a local bar association where you can find referrals for attorneys that specialize in real estate law or probate or any other type of law. If you are going to do any kind of creative financing, it would behoove you to have a real estate attorney who is skilled in the type of financing you are attempting to do look over and approve your contract. In fact, a clause in your contract that says, "Subject to Buyer's attorney's approval," could save you time and thousands of dollars.

If you are a beginning investor, an attorney or accountant should advise you about the type of entity in which to hold your properties. Some common types are trusts, LLCs, and partnerships, to name just three. This book does not address the pros and cons of how to hold title, yet it is a very important component of any real estate transaction. An attorney can save you thousands of dollars from frivolous lawsuits by ensuring that you hold title in the way that will best protect your assets.

Attorneys should also be consulted about unlawful detainer actions, evictions, and boundary disputes with neighbors. Unfortunately, these issues do arise from time-to-time where real estate is concerned and a good lawyer can, in most cases, direct you to a quick and equitable resolution.

As far as the other members of your team, like a home inspector, escrow officer, title officer, home warranty representative, contractors, and a geologist, you will begin building a network of these types of advisors as you dig into your first transaction. If there is a REALTOR® involved, he or she can direct you to competent people. If you are buying directly from an owner, you could still ask a REALTOR® or another investor for suggestions.

Faith without Works is Dead

A common question that comes up for people of faith is whether or not they should work exclusively with people who believe as they do. There are two extremes on this issue. I have heard more than one person say that they have been burned by people from their church and would never use anyone of faith again. On the other hand, some people say they will only work with people who believe exactly as they do. In Los Angeles, many people groups tend to live and work in the same area. It is not uncommon for these people to work with others who speak the same language or share the same culture as they do.

My opinion is that you should choose your team members based on their knowledge and experience. For instance, I have a broker's license that allows me to sell real estate in the entire state of California; however, that does not qualify me to broker a 100,000 square foot commercial building in Sacramento. One, it is way out of the area I serve. Two, I haven't done one commercial sale in eighteen years. In fact, I have never done a commercial sale. I would like to eventually own commercial property. When that time comes, I will be choosing a commercial specialist to represent me. A good commercial broker will save me substantially more money than he will cost. If I can find someone who shares my values, that's an even greater plus, but I am not going to make it the final criterion for whom I choose to represent me.

As you begin the process of building your team, ask God to lead you to the right people and believe that He has heard and is answering your prayer. You'll also find resources at www.RodneyJohnson.com to help in locating a good agent.

CHAPTER 5

Owing No Man Anything?

> Owe no one anything except to love one another, for he who loves another has fulfilled the law.
>
> (Romans 13:8)

> Let no debt remain outstanding, except the continuing debt to love one another, for he who loves his fellowman has fulfilled the law.
>
> (Romans 13:8, NIV)

When people read this verse, one of three things usually happens: they feel condemned because they have gone into debt; they feel hopeless because they think that it is against biblical principles to obtain a mortgage to buy a house; or they feel faith building inside because they are either on track to get out of debt or they have paid off their notes and are living debt-free.

Obviously, the goal is to be free of all encumbrances, yet I do not think we can categorically state that a person is sinning if they have a mortgage on their house that they can comfortably afford. The person who rents a house or apartment still "owes" their landlord a monthly check. By refinancing my mortgage last year, I lowered my payment for the next five years to a point where it would cost me an extra $1,300 per month to rent my own house. This amount is in addition to what my mortgage payment is.

Deuteronomy 28 is another famous passage that addresses the issue of debt. The first fourteen verses enumerate the blessings that will come upon the children of Israel if they are obedient to God. (By the way, Galatians 3:29 says that if you are Christ's then you are Abraham's seed, and heirs according to the promise. So, the blessings enumerated for Abraham's offspring are yours, too.) The last part of Deuteronomy 28:12 says, "You shall lend to many nations, but you shall not borrow." I feel confident giving to ministries who have taken a position that they will not go into debt to expand their buildings or land holdings. Because they are dependent on the giving of partners to cover their expenses, this is a prudent and biblically-based decision, which I believe God honors.

That said, let me point out here that if we look at the context of Deuteronomy 28 in its entirety, it appears that the blessings of the first part, and the curses listed thereafter, are progressive. We will be progressively blessed as we grow in obedience to the commands of God. Part of the blessing is we will prosper to such a point that it won't be necessary to go into debt. Instead, we will be the ones lending money to other nations.

My wife, Valerie, and I have just started this practice within the last year. Through our self-directed Individual Retirement Account (IRA), we made a loan to another person who needed money to fix up their property in order to sell it. We are now working with a mortgage company to fund another loan for a borrower who owns a duplex. It is gratifying to be in this position. Even so, we still have a mortgage on our primary residence. Our goal is to be mortgage-free on our personal home in the near future.

Investment properties are another matter in my opinion. If you own houses, apartments, commercial buildings, or other investment properties whose notes are covered by the rent payments received each month, I do not feel that you are violating either of these scriptures from Romans or Deuteronomy concerning debt. By keeping current with the beneficiary of the note you made on your investment properties, you do not "owe" them anything *pragmatically*. You are simply fulfilling the terms of the contract you made with the lender. The beauty of owning investment properties is that they can be properly leveraged with a corresponding mortgage and you will not only cover the payments each month, you will also have a positive cash flow that will provide you with income to pursue your goals.

Now, let me say also that it is possible to "over leverage" properties in an unwise use of other people's money to obtain investment properties. Furthermore, if you are pushing the limits on what would be considered by a qualified financial adviser a reasonable amount of debt in your investment portfolio, then you may be positioning yourself for a catastrophe if the local economy takes an unexpected turn or some other unforeseen event deprives you of your necessary cash flow. Again, I recommend the use of a team of sound professionals when making any real estate decisions— including investments—to be sure you keep your debt-to-income ratios balanced at a safe level.

Consequently, pragmatically speaking, I consider a person to be truly "in debt" when they cannot comfortably afford their monthly payments. I never encourage clients to buy a bigger house when it will stretch them past their financial comfort zone. In most cases, people who go from renting a house to purchasing will generally have to pay more per month due to a mortgage payment. Sometimes the payment comes close to their previous rent payment when you factor in the interest deductions that the government allows us to take on our tax return each year.

Caveat Emptor, Let the Buyer Beware

As a side note, I would be highly suspicious of an accountant who tells you that you "need" a mortgage on your primary residence in order to pay less in taxes. It does not make sense to me to pay one dollar in order to get a thirty cent tax break. Something's wrong with that picture.

Some preachers take a strong position that it is unbiblical for people of faith to borrow money. If God has spoken to you and told you not to go into debt, then do not be disobedient and take out a loan for a purchase. Likewise, if you are already in debt, do not limit the Lord with your words by saying, "I will never get out of debt." The goal should be to get to a point where you are the lender and not the borrower. Remember, the blessings of Deuteronomy 28 are progressive, so you need to be actively believing God for His promises to become a reality in your life–and working toward that goal with practical "works" that will make your faith effective.

Let me give you another example from my own life: a couple of years ago, my teenage son was driving an eleven-year-old car with over 100,000 miles on it. It was adequate at best. We had bought a nice used Audi for him; however, I was driving it myself until I could find a car to use in business. Needless to say, the pressure from my son to get myself a car mounted daily. I felt strongly that I was not to go into debt at that time for a car, so I resisted his pleas. After two or three months of cajoling, I was almost ready to cave one morning after another "Please Dad, get yourself a new car so I can have the Audi."

I went to prayer and told the Lord I was *really* feeling the pressure and asked what I should do. Immediately, Hebrews 10:35 came to mind, which says, "Cast not away your confidence, which hath great recompense of reward." What I heard in my spirit, was "Cast not away your <u>confession</u>, which has great recompense of reward." My confession had been up to this point: "I drive a debt-free car." I immediately made a decision to continue to believe this way. I didn't have to wait long. That afternoon a client called, told me that her dad had a Ford Explorer Eddie Bauer Edition that they were bringing back from Palm Springs, and asked if I would like to drive it for free for three months until they took it to their home in Idaho. Needless to say, I accepted their generous offer. An unexpected and added blessing was that they waited ten months to take the auto out of state.

My point in telling you this story is that obedience has its own rewards just as God promised in Deuteronomy 28. Additionally, as you learn to hear the voice of the Lord, He will lead you so that you are kept from a burden of "debt." Nevertheless, this story also illustrates that you need to be flexible in receiving His blessings, in any way the Lord chooses to bring them. The key point here is that debt is neither a sin, nor is it a necessity—just obey God and let His progressive blessings take you into your Promised Land.

CHAPTER 6

Seeing That Which is Yet Unseen

> Then He brought him outside and said, "Look now toward heaven, and count the stars if you are able to number them." And He said to him, "So shall your descendants be."
>
> (Genesis 15:5, 6)

Because God calls those things that be not as though they were, He has to have a vivid mental picture in mind before He ever speaks the creative word. Can you imagine the chaos that would ensue if God didn't know exactly what He was creating? However, we know from scripture that God is not the author of confusion; therefore, He has to know in advance precisely what He is making and how it will function.

In Genesis 15:5, 6, the Creator helped Abram get the picture of how many descendants he was going to have by showing him the stars and telling him to count them, if he was able. Obviously, it was impossible for Abram to count the stars with the naked eye. This visual aid of the stars was meant to get Abram's mind off the fact that he had no heirs at all and on to the promise of God. The great thing about this living word picture is that every evening Abram would look at the stars and again be reminded about God's promise three hundred and sixty-five days a year.

Can you imagine the excitement that must have grown in him

over a period of time as he looked at the sky each evening? Moreover, verse six says that he believed in the Lord, and He accounted it to him for righteousness. Many people make the mistake of saying, "I will believe it when I see it." Here we find Abram believing the promise *before* he actually saw it. I submit to you that had he not believed it before he saw it in the natural realm, he never would have seen it at all.

The success motivation field has known for years that you must see it in order to receive it. This is why those who train sales people encourage their protégés to cut out pictures of things they want to acquire and put them in a place where they will see them several times a day so that it will motivate them toward the achievement of their sales goals.

My father-in-law has been a trainer for years and tells this humorous story in his classes. Early in his sales training days, he told a class that they become what they think about the most. At this point, a man sitting on the front row raised his hand and said, "That is not true." Trying to be a diplomat, Dad asked him, "Why do you say that?" He replied, "If I became what I thought about most, I would be a woman." The class had a good laugh; however, I hope the man didn't miss the point my father-in-law was trying to make. There are other examples in the Bible in which God used word pictures. We will dig into one of those in short order.

No More Kicking Sand in the Face of this 98-Pound Weakling

First, I would like to share something that happened to me in January of 1998. Every year, I write down goals for things that I want to accomplish in the ensuing twelve months. Health and fitness are part of the goals that I address along with personal, family, business, financial and spiritual goals. In 1998, I wrote down something to the effect of "get in shape and lose twenty pounds." As I did most years, I would start out in January hitting the gym two to three times a week; however, as often occurred, I would burn out in very short order. Except this year, the Lord spoke to me in mid-January. He said, *"You do not see yourself as a strong man."* This was true.

In junior high, our physical education coach started a three-day-

58

a-week weight lifting program in the early morning hours before first period. I went at first but became intimidated by how much stronger the other guys were than me. What I failed to realize is that many of them had already built strong muscles bucking 100 pound bales of hay onto wagons every summer on their parents' farms. Since I lived in town and didn't have to do hard physical labor like that, my muscles hadn't had the opportunity to be developed naturally like some of my classmates. So, like Abram, I needed a new visual picture of myself.

My own personal count-the-stars-and-number-them-if-you-are-able-to moment didn't come until five months later. I was at work in late June when my fax machine kicked on and started spewing out pages about a weight training/change your body contest in just twelve weeks. My best friend, Gaylon, who was also a Midwest farm boy now living in California and had grown up throwing bales of hay onto wagons every summer, was the culprit behind this fax. I had shared with him earlier that month that I wanted to get into shape. Now he was throwing down the gauntlet to put up or shut up. I decided to put up since the grand prize was a new Corvette.

Once I read and saw how dramatically the previous year's winners had changed their bodies, I believed that I could do it, too. I began by immediately changing the way that I ate—both what I put in my mouth and when I ate it. Smaller portions, six times a day became the norm for me. Then I hired a trainer to put me on a program to build muscle and reduce fat. The sponsor of the contest also owned *Muscle Media* magazine, so I would buy it and learn as much as I could about changing my body. And it worked! Through getting a picture of myself as a "strong" man, I began to change.

In high school, my best friend once said to me in a moment of irritation that I probably couldn't bench press 100 pounds. To further compound my irritation with him, he was right. I couldn't. I had let that image from junior high weight training days color my perception of myself as a weak person instead of a strong person. However, once I saw that I could change myself dramatically in 12 weeks' time, I began to be able to lift heavier and heavier weights. I blew past the 100 pound bench press mark in no time flat. But the transformation all began with God's word to me in January, "You do not see yourself as a strong man." Once I got the right picture, other changes began to happen.

Get the Picture?

If you want to purchase or build your dream home or become a real estate investor, you must first get the right mental image. I had a celebrity client who built a 20,000 square foot home overlooking a lake tell me that they had a Christian couple visit their house. This visiting wife remarked that they too had a large home, which was so big that it took her 30 seconds to walk from the master bedroom to the kitchen. My celebrity client jumped out of his chair in mid-story and began timing the walk from his master bedroom to the kitchen and it was shorter than 30 seconds. Therefore, he rightly concluded that their visitors had one mammoth sized house.

I have heard this Christian couple testify about the process they went through in getting to the point where they could actually build the house. For years the wife would cut out pictures in magazines of rooms that she liked and keep them in a folder that she could refer back to. In fact, her husband related that she even got to the point of being a pretty good "country architect." By the time they were ready to build, she already had the house built and decorated in her mind. You may not need to go to that extreme but you do need to begin to see yourself as a homeowner or real estate investor, if that is your goal. (As a side note, they built their mansion debt-free).

One time a traveling preacher came to our church and asked how many people wanted to buy a house in the next year. Over 200 people raised their hands. (I should have handed out my business cards after the meeting). He proceeded to give them scriptures of promise to help build their faith. I wonder how many of them took those promises to heart and began to actively picture themselves as homeowners? I will bet the percentage was very low. I base that assumption on the fact that because I am a well-known part of the worship team, that I am probably the most visible REALTOR® in a church of over 10,000 members and I didn't get any calls from people asking, "How can I apply those promises in order to get my dream house?" Hopefully other agents in our church were able to help some of those people purchase their dream home.

I do know that one of our music ministers applied the promise and received his house, but I didn't hear of many others. How sad when the promises of God are "Yes and Amen," according to II Corinthians 1:20. They could have prospered in the ensuing three years as Southern California experienced 30 percent or more appreciation per year. However, far too often I hear people say, "I could never afford to live there," (meaning Southern California or any other place that is expensive). Remember Rich Dad's advice? Never say, "I can't afford it." Instead ask, "How can I afford it?" This will keep your mind open to receive God's promise.

God showed Abram a word picture to remind him of His promise. Throughout scripture our Creator uses building metaphors to help cement an image in our minds or in the mind of the person in the Bible. In telling of Abraham's triumphant faith in Hebrews 11, the writer recounts that Abraham "waited for the city which has foundations, whose builder and maker is God." My desire is to help you lay the foundation for your dream home(s) and be a good steward of all that God desires to give you. I am assuming you want to be like the man mentioned in Luke 6:48, "who dug deep and laid the foundation on the rock. And when the flood arose, the stream beat vehemently against that house, and could not shake it, for it was founded on the rock." In Isaiah 58:12, the prophet Isaiah prophesied that those who fasted for the right reasons would see "those from among you shall build the old waste places; You shall raise up the foundations of many generations; and you shall be called the Repairer of the Breach, the Restorer of Streets to Dwell In." This could be interpreted in both a literal and figurative sense.

Our inner cities are crying out today for people with a sense of mission to come in and become the restorer of streets to dwell in. On the other hand, a drug-addicted teenager living in a $3 million house in Beverly Hills needs someone to be the Repairer of the Breach on his behalf in order to help him overcome his addiction. These are examples of what the Lord could have been referring to when He told our congregation that He was giving us "spiritual real estate." Along with the *Glossary of Real Estate Terms* at the end of this book, I am also including a list of scriptures pertaining to houses and building so that you can increase your practical *and* spiritual knowledge.

Daddy, Will You Tell Me a Story?

Skipping ahead in Abraham's story, I imagine that after the son of promise, Isaac, was born he would often take little Isaac outside and point up in the evening sky toward the stars and recount how God promised him that his descendants would be as numerous as those luminescent lights. I can hear Isaac now, "Not again, Dad. You have told me this story a thousand times." However, once Isaac was grown and had twin boys of his own, I am sure he told them the same story over and over again. "Why," you might be asking, "do you think this?" It has to do with something that happened to Abraham's grandson, Jacob, while he was working for his father-in-law, Laban.

For those of you not familiar with Jacob, he agreed to work seven years for the right to wed Rachel, Laban's younger daughter. On the wedding night, Laban sent his older daughter, Leah, into Jacob's tent because he didn't think that it was right for the younger daughter to wed before the older one. Consequently, Jacob had to work another seven years for the right to marry his true love, Rachel. Throughout the years, God prospered Jacob and his herds grew exponentially even though Laban changed his wages ten times. Finally, Jacob had had enough of Laban's conniving ways and determined to leave him and return to his home country. Laban begged him to stay because he recognized that his flocks had flourished under Jacob's oversight. Jacob didn't want Laban to give him anything to coerce him to stay. Instead he made a suggestion as to how he would be compensated as delineated in Genesis 30.

So he said, "What shall I give you?"

And Jacob said, "You shall not give me anything. If you will do this thing for me, I will again feed and keep your flocks: Let me pass through all your flock today, removing from there all the speckled and spotted sheep, and all the brown ones among the lambs, and the spotted and speckled among the goats; and these shall be

my wages. So my righteousness will answer for me
in time to come, when the subject of my wages
comes before you: every one that is not speckled
and spotted among the goats, and brown among
the lambs, will be considered stolen, if it is with
me."

And Laban said, "Oh, that it were according
to your word!" So he removed that day the male
goats that were speckled and spotted, all the
female goats that were speckled and spotted,
every one that had some white in it, and all the
brown ones among the lambs, and gave them
into the hand of his sons. Then he put three days'
journey between himself and Jacob, and Jacob
fed the rest of Laban's flocks.

(Genesis 30:31-36)

What happened next sets the stage for a dramatic illustration of
why we need a vivid mental image of our desired goals. Jacob took
some poplar, chestnut and walnut branches and stripped the bark
off of them so that they looked streaked, spotted and speckled—just
like the kind of goats that were to be his pay. Then, when the strong
animals came to the place to drink water and mate, he would place
the spotted and speckled branches in front of them. Conversely, when
the weaker animals appeared, he took the branches away so that they
would not have the same visual stimulus as the stronger animals.
As a result of this practice, the strong goats produced spotted and
speckled babies and Jacob's herds increased dramatically, while his
duplicitous father-in-law's herds became weaker and dwindled in
number. Genesis 30 recounts this:

Now Jacob took for himself rods of green
poplar and of the almond and chestnut trees,
peeled white strips in them, and exposed the
white which was in the rods. And the rods
which he had peeled, he set before the flocks
in the gutters, in the watering troughs where
the flocks came to drink, so that they should

conceive when they came to drink. So the
flocks conceived before the rods, and the flocks
brought forth streaked, speckled, and spotted.
Then Jacob separated the lambs, and made
the flocks face toward the streaked and all the
brown in the flock of Laban; but he put his own
flocks by themselves and did not put them with
Laban's flock.

And it came to pass, whenever the stronger
livestock conceived, that Jacob placed the rods
before the eyes of the livestock in the gutters,
that they might conceive among the rods. But
when the flocks were feeble, he did not put them
in; so the feebler were Laban's and the stronger
Jacob's. Thus the man became exceedingly
prosperous, and had large flocks, female and
male servants, and camels and donkeys.
(Genesis 30:37-43)

Sometimes when Christians hear that they need to visualize the
desired outcome, they associate it with New Age thinking and other
cultic behavior. Yet, the Bible explicitly tells us that without a vision,
the people perish. I hope you can see from this Biblical example that
God wants us to picture the desired outcome ahead of time. In fact,
Revelation 13:8 says that Jesus was "slain from the foundation of
the world," which tells me that God knew we were going to sin and
had already made a way for us to be redeemed ahead of time. He
had a very clear picture of what He wanted for His creation. Do not
let the enemy of your soul steal a God-ordained tool that will bring
you into alignment with His plans and purposes for you to inherit
the land He desires for you to rule and reign over.

I finish this chapter with this thought from my father-in-law,
Harold Dyck, who says, "We are being drawn inexorably toward
that which we think about most." What are you thinking about in
relationship to your real estate goals? Before you move on to other
things, take a few minutes to reflect on what your real estate goals are
and create a vivid picture of the lifestyle you envision for yourself.

See in your "mind's eye" the type of house you want to live in. It would do you good to drive through areas in town where you would like to own rentals or commercial property sometime soon. Abraham looked at his word picture every night. It would behoove you to do the same.

However, it is important to note that the vision was not enough for Abram to receive the promise of God. There was a limiting factor in Abram's life that needed to be removed before God's plan could come to full fruition—and God had a plan for removing it. Contained within the unique method the Lord used to dislodge that barrier is a key for you and me to consider if we, too, want to fully possess the promises of God in our own lives...including our own Promised Lands.

CHAPTER 7

Names...and a Dog Called Bon Queesha

> No longer shall your name be called Abram,
> but your name shall be Abraham; for I have made
> you a father of many nations.
> (Genesis 17:5)

We saw in the previous chapter that God first showed Abram a picture of how numerous his descendants would be by daring him to number the stars. Now in this passage, which happened about thirteen years later, we see God doing something else to get Abram ready to receive the child of promise. Through the intervening years between these two points, people still called this nomad, Abram, which means "high father." However, with his name change, people were suddenly calling him "father of many nations." Now he was not only seeing the promise every evening in the sky, he was hearing the promise numerous times throughout the day as people called him "Father of Many Nations." No wonder he is known as the Father of the Faith.

As you think about the dreams that you have for your real estate goals, I encourage you to ask the Lord about your name. Have you ever looked up its meaning in a book of names? Over the last hundred years, we as a nation didn't pay much attention to the meaning of names like they did in biblical times. One of the most popular Christian books in the last few years has been *The Prayer of Jabez.* In the short passage describing this prayer, we learn that Jabez's name meant "He will cause pain." Hey, wouldn't you love to grow up with a name like Pain? It might work for a defensive lineman for a professional football team, but otherwise, I can't think of too many people who want to be known as the person who causes pain. I have a friend who's a chiropractor with the last name of Pane; however, his life work has been to help alleviate and relieve pain, not cause it.

Just for the Halibut…

My full name is Hal Rodney Johnson, II. I was named after my father, who goes by Hal. When my son was born, we named him Hal Rodney Johnson, III. We did not do this because of pressure from my folks. Instead, we had researched the meaning of Hal and Rodney and liked what they meant. Hal means "strong leader" and Rodney means "man of renown" or "famous island." Our desire in naming our son was that he would be a man of renown known for being a strong leader.

Because Daddy went by "Hal," I was called Rodney. I have to admit that as a teenager, I didn't particularly like my first name. I once had a girlfriend who thought my middle name sounded too British for her taste. After I reached my adult years and people would ask me why I didn't go by "Hal," I would joke, "I don't use that name because I got the *Hal* out." They would laugh and think how witty I was with my self-deprecating humor. However, self-deprecating humor is a slap in the face of our Creator who made us in His image. This truth was brought home to me about five years ago when I was attending a real estate seminar with my partner, Joseph.

After the sessions were over for the day, we began to pray together about our real estate careers. It was in this attitude of prayer that God very demonstrably showed me I was undercutting what He wanted to do in my life every time I made the joke about "getting the *Hal* out." He needed me to be a strong leader in our industry, yet I was thwarting his plans by my careless words. I repented immediately and have never made that joke again.

When I encouraged you to ask the Lord about your name, you

may have thought that you do not have a distinctive name that links specifically to your profession; however, allow the Holy Spirit to search you and see if you have called yourself names that are contrary to God's design for your life. Also, have other people called you names that you have taken upon yourself? Names like "Loser," "Lazy," "Good-for-nothing," "No-account," or even curse words like "Bastard," become an albatross around people's necks if they allow them to sink into their psyches. If you will search the scriptures, you will find that God uses words like "Destiny," "Future," and "Hope" to describe his plans for his people. Therefore, do not allow others to control your future by subscribing to their names of doubt and unbelief for you.

Dead Rotting Flesh

I had a real estate transaction with a buyer's agent a few years ago that started out on the wrong foot from day one. There had been multiple offers on the house and his clients had the strongest bid, so I encouraged my seller to accept their offer, which they did. However, within minutes of acceptance, he began to find things wrong that seemed to be sabotaging his own clients. After they completed their inspection of the house, he used inflammatory words to my seller like "extreme" in describing a slight sloping of the patio back toward the house at a one-quarter inch or less angle. As time went on, he kept finding more and more things to describe with inappropriate terms that were pushing our clients toward canceling the deal. It seemed like every phone call brought another negative characterization from this man.

Ultimately, it got to the point that after I had dealt with this man for two-and-a-half weeks, I couldn't take his negative talk anymore, so I turned him over to my partner, Joseph, who had the same experience. Hearing us vent about this agent's antics, my longtime assistant and buyer's agent, Robynn, pointed out that his name literally meant "dead, rotting flesh." Suddenly, it all became very clear to us. His name had become a curse to him and without realizing it, he was speaking death to virtually every situation in this deal.

I believe that had it not been for our prayers, the escrow never would have closed. Ultimately, it did close and our sellers sent a letter to the president of Century 21 praising Joseph and me for the job we did in getting their home sold under these very difficult circumstances. Had we realized upfront who we were dealing with, we could have started out on a different tact with this agent by leading him to see what was right with the transaction, rather than seeing everything from a negative perspective.

One of the pastors at my home church tells the story of naming her children and what happened pertaining to the meaning of their names. Her firstborn was named Brian, which means "strong." She and her husband wanted Brian to be strong in every sense of the word, both literally and spiritually. However, she relates that during his earliest years of life, he would cry at the drop of a hat and was anything but a strong little boy. They were concerned that they had a real wimp on their hands. Their youngest daughter was named Lindsey, which means "Yielded." She had been named this because they wanted her to be yielded to God in every aspect of her life. Again, they faced challenges with this child when in fourth grade it became apparent that if they didn't do something dramatic, they were in danger of losing Lindsey to the wrong influences. It took pulling her out of Christian school, no less, and home schooling Lindsey for a year to get her to the point of "yielding" to God's spirit.

Now I am happy to say that both Brian and Lindsey have matured into a "strong" young man and a "yielded," lovely young woman, respectively. In fact, one year ago Brian stood before 7,000+ people and gave a stirring eulogy to his father who had died unexpectedly at the age of 49. I have never seen anyone so poised and "strong" under those kinds of circumstances. Brian's grandfather also asked him to speak at a Promise Keeper's event in front of 15,000+ men. I would say you have got to be one strong young man to do that as a twenty-year-old.

Lindsey also showed her "yielded-ness" by not insisting on getting engaged as originally planned and choosing to live with her mother as they navigated the first year of life without a father and husband. I am sure that Brian and Lindsey would tell you that they are who they are today in large part because of the prayers that their parents and grandparents prayed for them, particularly that they become the prophetic meaning of their names.

I have got news for you. Like Brian and Lindsey, you have probably already been challenged about the meaning of your name and may not have even realized it. Whether it's your literal name or a moniker like "Liar," it's time for some soul searching.

Sticks and Stones, Yeah Right.

Early in my professional life, a woman at ABC made some remarks that directly reflected on the meaning of my name. After I had worked in the Prime Time Programming Department for two seasons, a Program Executive's position opened up. I had been reading scripts and writing synopses for our dramatic series and attending our weekly Current Program meeting for two years and was ready for a new challenge. I knew that they would probably want someone with more experience; however, I decided to show my initiative by analyzing a comedy script from one of the shows that the new Program Exec would be assigned to. I read the script, wrote my notes, made suggestions for improving it and gave it to the Director of Comedy for her perusal. She would be the first gatekeeper that I would have to pass in order to have a shot at the Program Exec's job.

When she called me in, the meeting started out pleasant enough; however, it quickly turned personal. While I respected her right to disagree with me about my notes for the script, when she said, "I really do not think you are leadership material," it got very personal. Just like Brian and Lindsey who were attacked at the heart of their names, I was being attacked at mine. Instead of showing true leadership and challenging her comment, I quickly and quietly left the meeting. Whoever said that sticks and stones may break my bones but names will never hurt me, didn't know what he was talking about. If accepted internally, names that others foist on you can cripple you for your whole life. Her words carried a curse that I allowed to alight for a period of time in my soul.

After I left ABC, I was able to share this incident with my spiritual father, Jack Hayford, and his prayer for me broke the initial curse and set me on the course of becoming a "strong leader" and a "man of renown." Pastor Jack's prayer was not the only thing that had to happen to release me into my calling and destiny; however, it was the start.

Since then I have further attempted to sharpen my leadership skills by listening to John Maxwell's monthly mentoring CD "Maximum Impact" for business people. I highly recommend John's program for the person wanting to learn more about leadership. You can also order any of John's great books on leadership by visiting my website at www.RodneyJohnson.com. Prayer and listening to anointed sermons and lessons are part of the keys that will release you into your next level of effectiveness in the kingdom of God.

"So how does this relate to real estate?" you might be asking. Far too many REALTORS® have a saying that they repeat over and over about buyers. The phrase, I am sorry to say, is "Buyers are liars." Unfortunately, it is a truism. Too many buyers pledge their loyalty to working with only one REALTOR® and then renege on that promise when it becomes convenient to buy a house through someone else. Consequently, agents feel justified in saying that all "Buyers are liars." I do not say that about the buyers that I work with because I realize that my words are important. My words have creative power. Since I can create with my words, why would I want to create an environment of mistrust by naming my buyer a liar?

Have you been named something that is holding you back from taking the first step to home ownership? Have parents told you that you'll never amount to anything? Has a relative told you that you are too slow to learn anything other than a menial trade? Have you told yourself not to have too high expectations so that you won't be disappointed? These self defeating words come with names like "Loser" and "Dummy" that we tend to appropriate more quickly than we do God's names for us.

Did you know that God is going to give you a new name someday? Revelation 2:17 tells us of that time. If you notice in the New Testament, people were given new names once they became Christians. Simon was named Peter, which means "rock." Jesus wanted him to get a picture of himself being a solid piece of granite that would not change under pressure. Like Abraham before him, Peter would grow into the prophetic meaning of his name as he heard people call him "rock" many times each day. Saul became Paul, which means small; little; humble. In fact, I heard a preacher say one time that the tradition of having a middle name grew out of the practice of Christians taking a new name once they had converted. If that is the case, then the enemy of our souls has succeeded in stripping something powerful from our lives. As for me, I am going to believe that I am a "strong leader" who is renowned for encouraging others to achieve their God-given purpose and destiny. Real estate is just one piece of the puzzle.

What's in a Name?

So getting back to real estate, why don't you think about taking the name "investor," or "homeowner," or "developer?" Even if you haven't bought your first home yet, have some business cards printed up with your dream name underneath your real name. My card reads: Rodney Johnson—Broker Associate. Yours could read: John Smith—Real Estate Investor. Mary Jones—Developer. When you start handing those cards out, people will start relating to you as you have named yourself and not how others from your past have named you.

If you are thinking, "But I am not a real estate investor," remember that God sees the end from the beginning. You need to start doing the same. Even before making my first million dollars, I decided to name myself a millionaire. I do not arrogantly go around telling people that, by faith, I am a millionaire, but in the privacy of my bathroom, I look in the mirror and say "I am a money magnet." "Money comes to me every day." I go so far as to proclaim how much money comes to me every month. If this kind of talk is scaring you, I challenge you again to do some soul searching and find out what "name" from your past is causing you to contend with what I have just written.

To reassure you, I do not love money because the *love* of money is the root of all evil. Money itself is not evil. Loving it is evil. I appreciate what money can do for a person. My goal is to have money working for me instead of me working for money.

If, while reading this chapter, you have sensed that others have

named you something other than what you are destined to become,
pray this prayer with me:

Father, I recognize that names are important. Forgive me
for the times I have cavalierly made comments about my name
without regard to the ramifications of my words. Forgive me
also for accepting names from other people who do not have a
clue about the plans You have for each of us, plans to give us a
future and a hope. I choose right now to turn and walk in a new
direction toward You and the name You have given me.

In the name of Your son, Jesus, I renounce the power that the
name _____ has had in my life. I break its hold over
me and declare in its place Your name for me. You have called me
Son (Daughter). You have called me Accepted in the Beloved. You
have called me "Overcomer." You have called me, "Victorious."
I choose to believe those names are my destiny. And I thank You
and praise You now for the victory that is mine.

I pray this in the name of Your Son, Jesus, our Creator.
Amen.

Sister, Sister

Next to my wife, Valerie, my sister, Ronda, is the woman whom
I most admire. Even though she lives in Missouri and I live on
the West Coast, we talk frequently on the phone. Many of those
conversations close with prayer for our children and for each other.
For many years, Ronda was given a name by the human resources
director that affected her ability to get a promotion with a major
Midwest utility company. She let the name "Drop-Out" become her
reality, and it was literally years before she moved from a clerical
position to management.

Men would be hired at her office and she would train them, only
to see them promoted to positions of authority within the company
that she was more than qualified and capable of handling. However,
managers in the human resources department kept telling her that
she was not qualified for those jobs because she didn't finish college.
After being passed over and passed over, Ronda realized that she had

been gifted to do more than her company was asking or allowing her to do.

Even though she had "dropped out" of college to get married and obtain her MRS. degree, she had the qualities that her superiors were looking for. The person doing the hiring just didn't recognize it yet. When she was finally given the chance to spread her wings, she soared like an eagle. Promotion followed promotion and, at one point in her career, she ended up being the Team Leader for the entire state of Missouri. She went from being named "Drop Out" to accepting names like "Encourager," "Mentor," "Negotiator," and "Prayer Warrior." That last name is probably the name she likes best, even though all four names are monikers she wears with a meekness and humility today.

During the years when Ronda was wearing the name "Drop Out" and being passed over for promotions, her family knew that her name really was "Eagle" and that she would soar once she received the chance to fly. If you see yourself in my sister's story, do not despair. Pray the prayer above and believe that God is calling you "Man of Faith" or "Daughter of Faith." Accept His positive affirmation of who you really are and see His desires become a reality in your life. Allow me, if you will, to call you "Land Baron or Baroness."

A Dog Called Bon Queesha? Huh?

By the way, as the title of this chapter indicates, I do have a dog named Bon Queesha. This beautiful, docile golden retriever was named by our children (What were we thinking when we let them do that?). I should have known better when five-year-old R.J. (Hal, III) named our poodle "Heidi" because she "hid" as soon as he put her down. Three-year-old Emily named her parakeet "Flyer" because it "flew" off of her shoulder when first placed there on Christmas morning (Good thing the animals didn't poop first, otherwise we might have been calling one of our pets "Pooper").

Well, back to naming our golden retriever. One of our life-long family friends was making up names one day and shouted out "Bon Queesha." When the kids decided on such a designation for our new puppy, Valerie and I decided that there just had to be a meaning associated with such an unusual name. We decided that "Bon" would be like the French word *bon* in bon appetite, which means "good." When it came to finding a meaning for "Queesha" we had to stretch the credibility a little bit. Val thought that the first four letters could stand for "Queen," while the *sha* could be short for "shamrock." Therefore, we have a dog that we affectionately refer to as "The Good Luck Queen."

Now, before anyone gets uptight about our pet's name, let me first share with you a quick point of clarity: I personally do not believe in luck. I believe in hard work and God's favor. "Bon Queesha" just happens to be the name of our beloved pet—who is a part of God's will for our family at this time. I hope also that her name serves as a reminder to the reader that in this serious endeavor we call real estate, it is good, proper, and healthy to have a sense of humor. So, please do not take offense at the name of our dog.

Remember that the name of Abraham's wife was changed from Sarai to Sarah, which means "Princess." Then, this "Princess" had a son who she named *Isaac*, which means "Laughter." It's okay to laugh. Moreover, may *you* have the last laugh at the devil that has been trying to name you anything but "Son or Daughter of God." Furthermore, if the Holy Spirit is bringing to your mind a name that you have called yourself (or that others have called you) that is not in alignment with his will, turn back to page 76 and pray the prayer to break its hold on your life.

I trust that throughout this chapter, I have driven home the importance of names and their potential effects on your life. Without question, you and I need to be sure that we only allow positive labels to influence our future. However, to be truly successful in life and, consequently, in real estate, let me assure you that you will also need to have an understaning of some other powerful biblical principles. So, as a member of the family who makes up bizarre names for dogs, I invite you to develop along with me *A Writer's Love of Words...*

CHAPTER 8

A Writer's Love of Words

This is My covenant which you shall keep, between Me and you and your descendants after you; every male child among you shall be circumcised; And you shall be circumcised in the flesh of your foreskins, and it shall be a sign of the covenant between Me and you.
Genesis 17:10, 11

In order to get Abram to the point of becoming Abraham, the father of many nations, God first had to point out a recurring word picture in the night sky to get him seeing himself as being able to procreate. Then the next step was to get other people in agreement by having them call him, "Father of Many Nations," through the name change to Abraham. The third step required something extremely personal for a man, and that was for Abraham to signify in his body that he was in covenant with the Most High God by circumcising himself and all males in his household. Some of you have to be thinking right about now, "What could circumcision have to do with buying real estate? I picked up this book hoping to learn how to make some more money, not get a lecture in hygiene or Jewish customs." If you bear with me, I will show you how it all ties together.

We've learned thus far that God wants us to rule and reign over land, i.e., the earth. In order to do this we need to see ourselves as people of destiny. The names that we call ourselves and allow others to call us are also instrumental in whether or not we obey the

commandment to have dominion over the place God has called us
to live and own property. In Genesis Chapter 15, God had already
performed His side of the covenant when He passed between the
halves of the heifer, the female goat and the ram. Now, here in
Genesis 17, he is asking Abraham to sign his name to the covenant
by irrevocably marking his body through the act of circumcision.
As I mentioned in chapter two, when a person initiates covenant,
he exchanges strengths for weaknesses. God was saying, "I will be
your strength. Where you are unable to procreate, I will endow you
with my creative abilities." For Abraham's part, he had to take the
organ at the heart of his creativity and sexual identity and pare away
the fleshy part that was not necessary. In the New Testament, the
Apostle Paul writes about a circumcision of the heart.

> In Him you were also circumcised with the
> circumcision made without hands, by putting off
> the body of the sins of the flesh, by the circumcision
> of Christ, buried with Him in baptism, in which you
> also were raised with Him through faith in the
> working of God, who raised Him from the dead.
> And you, being dead in your trespasses and
> the uncircumcision of your flesh, He has made
> alive together with Him, having forgiven you all
> trespasses, having wiped out the handwriting
> of requirements that was against us, which was
> contrary to us. And He has taken it out of the way,
> having nailed it to the cross. Having disarmed
> principalities and powers, he made a public
> spectacle of them, triumphing over them in it.
> (Colossians 2:11-15)

This last sentence speaks of the disarming of demon beings
(principalities and powers) and, in a later chapter, I will address
why there is contention so many times in real estate transactions.
For now, I draw your attention to the sentence that says He (Christ)
has "wiped out the handwriting of requirements that was against us,
which was contrary to us. And He has taken it out of the way, having
nailed it to the cross." In order to succeed in the superintending of

lands and buildings, we need to get rid of the superfluous. Egos mess up more real estate transactions than anything else I can think of.

Many times you will have parents trying to influence their children who are buying their first house by giving them wrong advice about how much to offer or what sort of terms to put in the contract. When challenged, too many of these parents will not back down because of ego. I have heard a parent say, "Well, we didn't have to provide that kind of information to a lender when we bought a house, so why should my kids?" To them I would say, "Times have changed and so have lender requirements. If you want your kids to have a house, they will have to give the information to the lender or obtain a loan from you. Which would you prefer?" I do not mean to come off sounding harsh or uncaring; however, for those who call themselves Christians, there needs to come a paring away of the fleshy ego, a circumcision, if you will.

We also see in this passage from Colossians that the enemy of our souls has written down a list of requirements by which he could accuse us. The great thing is that Christ has wiped out those "handwritings" and nailed them to the cross. When we go back to the scripture at the beginning of this chapter, we notice that Abraham's response to entering into a covenant with God was to circumcise himself and every male in his household. Circumcision was Abraham's signature on the covenant which he made with God—a permanent signature, never to be altered. This is the way that people viewed a covenant in Abraham's time. As I mentioned earlier, only death could break a covenant. Like the passage in Colossians talking about a spiritual circumcision, Abraham's circumcision was a physical reality representing a spiritual truth. This is why it is so important to do something physical when you make an important decision. Obviously, I am not advocating that you be circumcised because you have decided to become a real estate investor; however, I am strongly suggesting that you do something physical to seal your decision. For instance, Habakkuk 2:2 says, "Then the LORD answered me and said: 'Write the vision and make it plain on tablets, that he may run who reads it.'" People of all religious beliefs understand the power of the written word. So, if you decide to become a real estate investor or a homeowner, write down your statement of purpose. I have heard testimony after testimony of people who have done this very thing and then been amazed when the very things they wrote down came into being.

Going to the Chapel and We're Gonna Get Married

After I moved to Los Angeles in January 1981, I didn't go home to Missouri until Christmas twelve months later. During that time of year-end reflection, I wrote down my goals for 1982, one of which was to meet a nice girl and enter into a relationship with her. I didn't have anyone in mind, except that my ultimate goal was to get married. Upon returning to Los Angeles, I continued the routines I had established the previous year, one of which was going to church at The Church on the Way and participating in their College Career Sunday school class. It was there that I met my future wife less than two months later. We were engaged in May of 1982 and married on December 30 of the same year.

In the fall of 2003, I attended a real estate seminar whose guest speaker was Glen Purdy. If you ever have the chance to hear Glen speak, by all means do so. He will inspire you with his enthusiasm and knowledge of the real estate market. During one of his sessions, he was also talking about the importance of writing things down. His "a-ha" that there really is something to writing down a specific statement of purpose happened when he wrote down a several-page job description of the perfect assistant. He wrote line after line of qualities and abilities that this person should have in great detail. Amazingly, less than three days later, the woman possessing all of the abilities he wanted in an assistant walked into his office.

Mega-mansion builder, Frank McKinney, reveals in his book *Make it Big!: 49 Secrets for Building a Life of Success* that he writes down his goals at the beginning of each week. Then, at week's end, he reviews them to see which ones he accomplished and sets more goals for the upcoming week. At the end of the year, he takes all of the week's goals and reviews them while planning for the upcoming year. I have followed Frank's advice and I write down my goals each week and review them daily.

I marvel sometimes at the things that happen to me that have no other reason for happening other than the fact that I wrote them down. I would encourage you to write down your goals. Be specific. For instance, if you want to buy five single-family houses this year, write it down. If you want to invest in a four-unit apartment building, write it down. If you want to form a partnership to buy larger properties, write it down. Like Abraham of old, you are putting your identity on the line when you actually write it down. You are saying, *This is what I intend to do. This is my statement of purpose. I was meant to rule and reign in this life and I am showing my intention by writing it down.* By the way, you can purchase Frank's book by logging onto my website at www.RodneyJohnson.com and clicking on *Rodney's Recommended Reads!*

I mentioned earlier that real estate is referred to in the opening verse of Genesis. It is also discussed in the closing chapter of Revelation. We also see that God told people to write His word. Moses wrote the first five books of the Bible. In fact, God thought it was so important to write down His word that He physically inscribed the ten commandments on tablets of stone, not once but twice. In Revelation 1:11, Jesus tells John "What you see, write in a book and send it to the seven churches which are in Asia." Again, we see the command to write things down. I believe this is one of the keys to releasing the desired intent. When we write something down, it signals our mind that an important message has been delivered. It then goes to work to bring about the desired result. Rarely will you find successful people who have not first written down their goals. God's *rhema* word to you is certainly important and should be preserved by writing it down.

The Crucible

I recently listened to John C. Maxwell's lesson for leaders called "The Crucible." John says that any great leader will usually go through more than one period of intense testing that will show what he or she is made of. He says that it won't make your character, it will reveal it.

In 1993, I had a crucible experience that had started the year before. When I got into real estate in February of 1987, the Southern California real estate market was in high gear. Prices were appreciating 20 percent or more per year. By 1990, that trend was reversing as more and more properties came on the market and major industries began leaving the area in droves. Because I hadn't paid close enough attention to the trends, I saw my income cut almost in half in 1992 because houses were not selling. Many sellers were upside down in their mortgages and could not afford to bring cash in to close the deal. Some were asking the lenders to accept a short pay-off in lieu of foreclosing.

It was in this environment that I went to my broker at the end of 1992 and told him that I wanted to solicit banks for the listings on their foreclosed properties (REOs). REO stands for Real Estate Owned and is what most lenders classify their foreclosures as. With his financial backing for six weeks, I hired Robynn Creitz for four hours a day and told her that our goal was to get at least three lenders who would use me in an ongoing basis to market their foreclosures. I had written down my objective. Now our job was to market to the lenders in hopes of getting approved to list their REOs.

January became February, February became March, March became April, and April became May without one listing from a bank. Having only closed two escrows thus far in the year, I was to the point of having only enough money left for the next forty five days if I cashed in my paltry IRA. Then we were looking at having to broach the subject of bankruptcy, which I didn't want to do. Over the previous year-and-a-half, we had accepted gifts and loans from both sets of parents; however, we were determined not to go back to them again. Consequently, in May of 1993, Valerie and I found ourselves sitting in the office of Jim Nelson, one of our assistant pastors who was the overseer of the church benevolence fund. Tears streamed down my face as I explained the predicament we found ourselves in and how we had gotten there with the downturn of the real estate market. When Pastor Jim offered to pay for our health insurance for the next three months through the benevolence fund, I was truly humbled and yet grateful at the same time.

Before we had gone into that meeting, I had received a call a few days before from Bank of America asking me to interview with one of their asset managers, a person who oversees the inventory and selling of the bank REOs. God gave me favor with the asset manager, and within a matter of days after meeting with Pastor Jim, I had my first listing, a $500,000 tri-level in Encino, a very desirable area in the south central part of the San Fernando Valley. Today, ten years later, this same house would sell for over a million dollars. This property sold immediately, leading to more listings from Bank of America.

By July, I was approved with Countrywide, another large nationwide lender. Smaller banks followed suit and in the last seven months of 1993, I made more money than I had in any previous twelve-month period. In 1994, even with a major earthquake rocking the Southland on January 17, I made almost double what I had earned in 1993. I submit to you that if I had not written down my objectives and put my identity on the line at the beginning of 1993, I would not have prospered and flourished like I did. You, too, need to write down your financial and real estate goals and look at them every day. Use the written word to create a mental picture of what you desire. See yourself as having already achieved what your written goals are.

"Trinspire" Me

Several years ago I began collecting three-word phrases that we use in every day conversation. When I saw how often we use three-word phrases in conversation, I recognized the motivational potential of these pithy aphorisms. I was specific about the types of three-word phrases in my collection. I wanted inspirational statements that would spur me and anyone who read or heard them to take some kind of positive action. Some of the first phrases that I collected and wrote down were "Take the shot," "Dare to Dream," and "Write It Down." As I collected more and more, I realized there was commercial potential with them if I expanded the concept. So, I coined the word Trinspiration™, which means a three-word phrase of inspiration or encouragement. Here is my Trinspiration™ for "Write It Down."

Write It Down

Lest you forget, write it down.

Lest your vision lose its clarity, write it down.

Lest you get to the end of a month, a year, or a life without accomplishing what you were destined to accomplish, write it down.

Words have power and when we can see those words, as well as hear ourselves speak them, faith begins to come to our hearts.

You are destined for greatness. Dare to dream and then write it down.

Write down the revelation and make it plain on tablets so that a herald may run with it. (Habakkuk 2:2)

As you can see, I am taking my own advice and writing down my ideas. If you would like to see more sample Trinspirations™, visit my website at www.RodneyJohnson.com where you can download the latest. Also, be watching my website for more information on when the Trinspiration™ book and computer screen downloads will be available.

I have touched on goal setting throughout this chapter but haven't given you specific actions to take because there are many fine programs for goal setting. I can think of none better than my friend Jim Rohn's series "The Art of Exceptional Living." This, too, can be ordered from my website when you click on the Jim Rohn link. Before you read another page, stop and write down your goals for the next seven days as a way of getting into the habit of writing things down. Maybe one of your goals is to order Jim's series. You, too, can develop a love of words and a love for *The Word* as you write down the things that God would show you about your purpose and destiny. You will find out His promises for you by reading what He has had "written down" in the book we call *The Bible*.

However, even if we're calling ourselves the name that God has given us, writing down our vision, and saying and doing all of the "right things," sometimes we may find ourselves in a situation that just stinks. The Bible promises that persecution will come because of the Word's sake, so even when we are on track with God's principles, opposition from the enemy will sometimes come. Therefore, do not despair if everything is not perfect in your life.

Furthermore, if you are under the misconception that my life has been all "hunky dory" throughout my days, I can assure you that it has not. I, too, have experienced setbacks and challenges from time to time. Therefore, to illustrate how to obtain the blessings of God despite the opposition from the enemy, I invite you to turn the page to see *What Job and I Had in Common.*

CHAPTER 9

What Job and I Had in Common

> And it came to pass, when he was close to entering Egypt, that he said to Sarai his wife, "Indeed I know that you are a woman of beautiful countenance. Therefore it will happen, when the Egyptians see you, that they will say, 'This is his wife'; and they will kill me, but they will let you live. Please say you are my sister, that it may be well with me for your sake, and that I may live because of you."
>
> (Genesis 12:11-13)

> Now Abraham said of Sarah his wife, "She is my sister." And Abimelech king of Gerar sent and took Sarah... Then Abimelech said to Abraham, "What did you have in view, that you have done this thing?" And Abraham said, "Because I thought, surely the fear of God is not in this place; and they will kill me on account of my wife."
>
> (Genesis 20:2, 10, 11)

Not once but twice Abraham lied to royalty about his relationship with his wife Sarah. While it is true that they were technically half-brother and sister, the reality is that they were husband and wife. From what we read in scripture, Sarah was one fine looking woman, too. She was so fine that kings desired to take her into their harems. I suppose that Abraham could be excused for his behavior. No, he couldn't. You see, Abraham's real problem was fear. That becomes very clear in verse 11 of chapter twenty when he says, "...they will kill me on account of my wife." Had he been secure in the terms of his covenant that God would protect him, he would not have succumbed to telling half-truths about his relationship with Sarah.

Fear is the biggest killer of faith. In fact, it is the total opposite of faith. It is a belief that the worst can and will happen. I have heard motivational speakers use the acronym of FEAR as False Evidence Appearing Real. While Abraham operated in fear twice when it came to being honest about who his wife really was, it is comforting to know that he grew to the point where he became known as the Father of Faith. So for those of us who haven't fully arrived yet at eradicating fear from our lives, do not give up hope. Ask God to overflow you with his perfect love because the Bible says that perfect love casts out fear. When situations arise that tempt you to fear, stand on that word and say out loud, "I will not fear because I have been filled with the perfect love of God and His perfect love casts out fear."

The Circle of Life Has Economic Circles, Too

As a novice real estate agent, I made the mistake of telling a person relocating to the Los Angeles area in 1987 that Southern California prices never go down. I naively thought they would just keep appreciating. However, by the time 1990 came to an end, we were already starting to see prices coming down. As more properties came on the market and businesses closed their doors in our area, prices continued dropping. By 1992, approximately 50 percent of the sales in the Southern California area were being driven by foreclosure sales. The banks were repossessing many properties and, if they didn't sell in 30 days, they would reduce the prices until they sold. In the process, this forced the prices down across the board.

Now, had I been living free of fear I could have increased my portfolio dramatically during the 1990's by purchasing many of these distressed properties. Instead, I saw that I had been wrong about California being outside the real estate cycles that the rest of the country routinely experiences. Therefore, I allowed fear to keep me from buying anything until 1999 because I was afraid that prices would never come back. Many people felt the same way and, like me, did not benefit from the dramatic comeback Southern California did experience in the late nineties and into 2005 at the time of the writing of this book.

I have made a decision, though, that I am not going to let fear dictate anything to me any more. Had I been actively seeking the Lord about what to buy in the 1990's, I am confident that He would have directed me to any number of properties. Even though I allowed a decade to pass without purchasing a single house when some of the best bargains were available, I choose not to live in the past but to learn from my mistakes.

I remember going to a men's meeting at my church toward the end of 1992 when I had experienced such a dismal year in sales and hearing another REALTOR® who specialized in apartment buildings say that he had asked the Lord at the beginning of 1992 where the real estate market was going. He testified that God showed him that the market was going to be driven by foreclosures so he positioned himself early as a specialist in the foreclosure market for apartment buildings and made in excess of $300,000 that year. Moreover, he also began to put together friends and relatives to purchase some of these bargain properties, as well.

After hearing this man speak, I went to my broker and told him that I wanted to be our office agent who listed bank owned properties as I wrote about in the previous chapter. If you will ask the Lord to remove fear from your life, He will be free to speak to you about what your real estate investments should look like. He can draw you to areas that are going to experience appreciation.

In just the last two weeks, two different people have given me unsolicited information about an area in Northern California that they believe is poised for a major breakthrough in real estate values. The Bible says that in the mouth of two or more witnesses a thing is confirmed. I haven't jumped in the car just yet to go buy property there; however, I do take both of these people's recommendations seriously and will make it a point of prayer.

The other night I arrived at my daughter's volleyball league playoff game an hour-and-a-half early. Since I had time to spare (notice I didn't say time to *kill*), I decided to drive through the neighborhood and go get some dinner. This area of Los Angeles has very expensive homes, yet, as I was driving, I sensed that the Lord really wanted to speak to me about positioning me here. I prayed for the people in that neighborhood. I prayed that they would have a chance to hear the gospel and respond to it. I also quieted myself before the Lord and believe He gave me some direction to take professionally. When I got home after the game, I immediately went to a real estate website and made an inquiry into something I had sensed in my spirit that I was to do. Had I been controlled by fear, I wouldn't have heard His voice, let alone had the faith to believe I could be a player in this particular market. I have taken the first step and await the next thing that he would have me do.

What is so freeing is that I can do this without fear of failure because if He has truly called me to this area, then faithful is He who called you (me) and He will perform it. That's scripture, by the way.

The Virtuous Woman is a Landowner

I particularly want to say to women who are reading this book that you can and *should* be leading when it comes to building a real estate portfolio. Chapter 31 of Proverbs, which has been dubbed "The Virtuous Woman Chapter," says, in describing her attributes in verse 16, that "she considers a field and buys it; from her profits she plants a vineyard." This is obvious to me that women are gifted to see deals and profit from them. One of my clients is a single mom and is one of the bravest women I know when it comes to investing in real estate. Every two years she is calling me to sell her house, take her tax-free capital gain and go buy another property as her principal residence. First it was a townhouse. Then she bought a real fixer upper, which she made look great. Her third house was brand new construction. Who knows what her next one will be!

I have noticed that in most real estate organizations the top producing agents are women. In the Century 21 system of which I have been a part for over 18 years, women are perennially the top producing agents and teams year in and year out. I believe that some have knowingly and others unwittingly tapped into the gifting that

90

God has placed on women to rule and reign over real estate.

One particular top female agent sells multiplied millions of dollars worth of properties and then turns around and gives back to her community by donating buildings to her church. Additionally, she takes off every Saturday and goes through her neighborhood talking to children about coming to Sunday school. The next day she sends a bus into the same neighborhood to pick up those children and take them to church.

While you may not be called to be a real estate agent, you are called to be "salt and light" to the world—to your realm of influence. Your real estate investments can provide one of the means to satisfy that commandment. If what I have just written resonates with your spirit, yet fear is rearing its ugly head again and whispering that you can't do it, do not submit to that spirit of fear. Begin to saturate your mind with the Word of God. At the end of this book, I have included "Mind Renewing" scriptures that will get your thoughts off of yourself and on to what a mighty God we have. You'll find scriptures like:

> For God has not given us a spirit of fear, but of power and of love and of a sound mind.
> (2 Timothy 1:7)

> You are of God, little children, and have overcome them, because He who is in you is greater than he who is in the world.
> (1 John 4:4)

I would be so bold as to say that you should write these scriptures out by hand and carry them with you. As I discussed in "A Writer's Love of Words," there is a power released when we write something down. If you want to quickly eradicate fear from your life, write down the scriptures that deal with this issue and review them throughout the day. Did you know that the Bible tells us 62 times in the King James Version to "fear not." Obviously, fear is a BIG problem.

The Thing I Greatly Feared Has Come Upon Me

I wish I had been doing this on a daily basis about five years ago. At that time, I had listed a house for two wonderful people for whom I had previously sold three houses. Their current residence was just an interim purchase that they had lived in after the 1994 earthquake while they built their 15,000 square foot dream home. For some reason, I allowed a gnawing fear to take hold in my mind, a fear that the house would not sell and that they would list it with someone else. Not only would I lose the sale, I would lose them as clients. Guess what? Like Job who said, "The thing I greatly feared has come upon me," I lost the listing and someone else did sell it. Fortunately, I did not totally succumb to fear and I have still retained these folks as friends. I am learning to live free of fear, and that should be everyone's goal.

If fear is stopping you from moving forward in acquiring real estate or doing something else that you know God has called you to do, then pray this prayer with me:

Father, I thank You that You have not only told us to live free of fear but You have also made a way to accomplish it. I ask that Your perfect love would become rooted and grounded in me to the point that I know that I know that I know You love me and, consequently, fear has no place in my life. When I am tempted to give in to fear, remind me of Your love. When I seem paralyzed to take action, remind me as You did Joshua of long ago that this book of the Law shall not depart from my mouth and that I shall meditate in it day and night to observe to do according to all that You have written in it. For then I will make my way prosperous and then I will have good success.

Thank You for eradicating fear from my life so that I am free to be and do all You have called and anointed me to do.

I pray this in the name of my fearless Savior. Amen.

Abraham finally got to the point where he could live free of fear. In fact, he grew to the level of faith in his God and faith in his covenant with Him that he could fearlessly tie his promised son to an altar and raise a knife to kill him because he knew that God would have to bring him back from the dead. You may not yet have that kind of faith in your covenant; however, let me encourage you with this comforting promise from Jesus' own mouth:

Do not fear, little flock, for it is your Father's good pleasure to give you the kingdom.
(Luke 12:32)

Furthermore, let me encourage you also by sharing the "formula" for experiencing a tremendous life...

CHAPTER 10

Trust - Fear = A Great Way to Live

> Now the Lord had said to Abram: "Get out of your country, from your father's house, to a land that I will show you. I will make you a great nation; I will bless you and make your name great; and you shall be a blessing. I will bless those who bless you, and I will curse him who curses you; and in you all the families of the earth shall be blessed."
>
> So Abram departed as the Lord had spoke to him.
>
> (Genesis 12:1-4a)

We have learned that eighty-seven-year-old Abram believed God that he would have a son and it was credited to him as being righteous. If you are going to superintend properties, you will have to learn to trust. Even a person who does not believe in God as Abraham did will have to learn to trust *people* at the very least if they want to acquire real estate. As I detailed in the opening chapter about the Hargitay's two-day escrow, we all had to trust many people. We had to trust the lender to fund the loan, the title company to properly record the deed, the escrow officer to make sure that all of the details were in order, Jorge to oversee the funding of the second mortgage, and a host of other people. For the Hargitays and myself, we had to trust God to make it all come together in very short order. People who are not trustworthy make life miserable for everyone else involved in a real estate transaction.

In Stormie Omartian's bestseller, *The Power of a Praying®* *Husband*, I wrote about two clients who were polar opposites in the area of trust. The first couple is Ty and Edie. They have been family friends since before my youngest was born, so it has been more than thirteen years that we've known them. Our friendship was forged in a church home group that they led during the early part of the 1990's. They prayed for us as a struggling young couple attempting to make our way in the real estate field when the income was uncertain from month to month.

Both Ty and Edie worked in radio at the time we were attending their home group. Ty had formed a radio syndication company that was doing quite well. Edie was working out of the home writing scripts for radio count down shows. In the late 1990's, Ty's company was bought out by a huge conglomerate who kept him on overseeing the sales department. It was in this context that he called and said that they would like to buy in a specific development in the Southwest valley. Ironically, it was in this very same development that a certain *Doo Wap Ditty* wasted my time for one year and then cut me out of a very large commission when he finally decided to purchase. I will go into the specifics of why there is contention in many real estate transactions in a later chapter.

I set a time with Ty and Edie to look at resale homes in this development, and to also show them the models. The builder was nearing the completion and only had a few new houses left. We started off our day looking at the resales. We looked at a children's game show host's house among others. I remember Ty commenting about the entry at one house. He thought that the swirling, chocolaty covered walls were reminiscent of being inside the middle of a coffee *Frappuccino®*. One of the reasons I liked working with Ty and Edie was their sense of humor. As you go about building your real estate team to help you acquire properties, make sure you have people with whom you feel comfortable.

After we had viewed the available resales, I took them over to the model homes area. It was at this point that Ty really started to get excited about what he saw. He started selling Edie on the possibilities

96

of this one particular model. In fact, he sold so hard and so long that another buyer came in and put a deposit down for that last floorplan while we were outside the sales office. Needless to say, he was a little disappointed. To top it off, they were scheduled to leave in a few days for a three-week vacation in Europe.

It was at this point that their trust in me really came to the forefront. Ty believed that they were to live in this development, so he put his money where his mouth was. Before leaving for Europe, he wrote a $30,000 check payable to my firm and gave me a notarized power of attorney to buy that model home in case it fell out of escrow while they were gone. Having someone put this kind of trust in you to help them fulfill their plans and dreams carries with it a big responsibility and yet it also is very rewarding from an emotional standpoint.

While they were in Europe, a house with a different floorplan fell out of escrow. When I went to inspect this house, I discovered that the potential buyer had spent a great deal of money on upgraded tile flooring throughout most of the downstairs. The person who chose this tile had a very particular taste in decorating, and it was not one that I particularly appreciated. However, as a broker, I have learned to sublimate my own tastes and do what the client wants. The pattern of the tile was not something that I could adequately describe via a telephone call to Ty and Edie, so I enlisted the help of the designer for the builder to make a video with me. I shot each room with my camcorder and had the designer do the voiceover, elaborating with much detail about what had already been put in each room. She did a great job.

Unfortunately, when my video caught up with them in Ireland, it took four hours to find a place that had a compatible system that could play it for them. Moreover, it had no sound and the color was off quite dramatically. Even with all of this working against us, Ty said to reserve the house with an option to cancel if they did not like what they saw once they were inside the house.

When they returned home, we went back to the development. Once inside, they decided that they did not like the colors of the tile, either. The video had not truly conveyed what was inside the house. However, not once did they feel that their money was in jeopardy because they knew they had someone working for them who was trustworthy. We walked back across the street to the sales office where we learned that a larger home had become available and that they could choose their own flooring. They made a decision on the spot to purchase that house and have been there ever since as of the date of this writing.

Opposites Do Not Always Attract

On the opposite end of the spectrum is a woman whom I will call Susie Won. Ms. Won called me because she had seen me on my cable television commercials, and "had a good feeling about me." She had power of attorney to sell two houses, so we listed both of them and in short order both of them received offers. That was when the trouble started.

Even though she "trusted" me to list them, her trust evaporated almost as quickly as it started. She would show up at our office without an appointment and demand to see me or one of my assistants if I was not there. We would go over and over with her what all of the documents meant that she was signing. Still she would be belligerent and had all of us walking on eggshells when she came to the office or called on the phone.

The real problems started when the vacant house belonging to her divorced husband sold. Though they were no longer married, he still gave her power of attorney to sell on his behalf because of his travel outside the country. When we received the preliminary title report, the title officer wanted to know why a certain woman's name was listed as a co-owner and more importantly as a "spouse" of the divorced owner. Susie knew this woman and tried to convince me and the title officer that in her country the word "spouse" actually meant a "good friend." Uh huh. Moreover, she claimed that this woman was somewhere in Europe and could not be reached. This particular house never closed because the title company would not insure it—and rightly so.

A month or two after Susie was out of our lives, my broker called me at home on a Sunday night to tell me that Susie was being profiled on the CBS program, *60 Minutes*. It seems that they were exposing 20th Century slave traders in America and she was being indicted for bringing women to the United States and forcing them to work as indentured servants for her and her diplomatic friends. (The "spouse" who was on title to one of the houses was one of those people).

In court, it was alleged that she forced these women to crawl on their hands and knees to serve her and her guests. In addition to the humiliation she foisted on them, she also took out credit cards in their names and ran up huge balances which she never paid. It was because of this that she was convicted and sent to prison. The *Los Angeles Times* reported that the judge would not let her go home to say goodbye to her teenage son because he feared that she would flee the country. The last I heard she was still serving time in prison.

Now, I recognize that these are two extremes when we compare Ty and Edie's trust with Susie's lack of it. Most people will fit somewhere in between and hopefully closer to the Ty and Edie end of the spectrum. As I mentioned in the beginning of this chapter, you will have to trust people in a real estate transaction. In order for Abram to receive his real estate gift, he had to leave the comfort of the known and launch out into the unknown. His trust was tested many times. Too many times people fail to achieve their dreams because they doubt that God has spoken to them. Consequently, they do nothing and stay in the land of the safe and comfortable. If you are trustworthy, you undoubtedly find that good things will come to you. For those who will trust God, too, they will see some awesome things happen.

"What Did You Say, Lord?"

When Valerie and I were looking to buy our first home in 1988, I had only been in real estate for about a year-and-a-half. Lenders then wanted to see two years' tax returns in the same line of work, which I didn't have. So, the only way I could get a conventional loan was to do what was called an easy doc application. This type of loan was based on a good credit score and did not require tax returns, hence the term "easy doc." At that time, to get this type of loan, you needed to put 25 percent down or find a seller who would carry a second loan.

Around the end of July, we found a house in our neighborhood that had been inherited by a brother and sister. It was only a two-bedroom one-bath house, and they were asking $210,000. Even though the price seemed high, the 10,000 square foot lot had the potential of being split and the sister indicated her willingness to carry a second loan. We had saved enough for a ten percent down payment and needed the siblings to carry a 15 percent second so that we could qualify for the easy doc loan on the first.

By the way, Valerie was pregnant with our second child who was due the first week of September. It was under these conditions that I drove by the house one day after we had made our offer. As I passed the street, I heard the Holy Spirit speak to me again about real estate. He said, "Give your 30-day notice." I knew that He meant to tell our landlord that we would be moving in 30 days even though we didn't have a solid deal to buy this house.

When I got home, I goofed in my spiritual leadership with Valerie. Instead of saying, "The Lord told me to give our 30-day notice," I said, "We need to pray about giving our 30-day notice." While this sounds nice and politically correct, I needed to lead the way in our obedience to what I had heard. Hey, when you are eight months pregnant and you don't have a definite place to move, it probably does not seem like God would tell you to move, especially if you didn't know where you were going. Except that is exactly what God told Abram to do—move to a land that He would show him.

Right on the heels of the decision not to give our notice, the siblings decided not to sell us their house because the brother wouldn't carry the second. At the time, it seemed that we had done the prudent thing by not giving our landlord notice. About two weeks later in the middle of August, I ran into a friend at church who puts together investment groups to buy real estate. We talked about the overheated market and then said our goodbyes. The next morning he called me and said, "Rodney, when I saw you yesterday the thought popped into my mind that I should have sold you this house that we have in escrow in West Hills. Well, this morning the buyer called and said that he was getting a divorce and didn't want to go forward with the purchase."

He went on to say that the house had four bedrooms, two baths and he would sell it to me for $169,000. Not only that, they would carry the entire loan for two years, so I wouldn't have to put any money down or qualify for a conventional loan. Valerie heard me say to my friend, "I'll take it. Where is it located?" Immediately, she began to ask questions. I said, "We've just bought a four-bedroom house that is twice the size of the house we were looking at purchasing for $41,000 less than we were going to spend." The kicker was that they wanted us to make our first payment on September 1, which would have been right on schedule for me giving our 30-day notice. By not trusting what I heard the Spirit say, it cost us an extra month's rent.

There's a saying that we live and we learn. However, I hope you will learn from my mistakes and not have to make all of them yourself. It is too expensive to have to make all of the mistakes ourselves, so learn from the mistakes and experiences of others. Jim Rohn says that it is too bad that failures do not give seminars. That way we could go and pay them to learn what *not* to do.

Maybe you are sitting there recalling an incident where you did something that caused an important person in your life to lose trust in you. If you haven't asked for forgiveness, then go to them now and admit that what you did was wrong. Ask for their forgiveness. If at all possible, go with a plan on how you can "right the wrong" you perpetrated. Then know that if trust has been destroyed, it will take time for it to be renewed.

If you have not yet started building your trustworthy real estate team, I would recommend that you start by asking for referrals from people whom you trust who have been successful in the real estate field. Remember that James, the brother of Jesus, reminds us "we have not because we ask not." So do not be afraid to ask.

In fact, let me add to that last admonition another: do not be afraid to give either. Why? Because therein is the "hidden" key to obtaining everything you want...

CHAPTER 11

How to Get Everything You Want

> Then Melchizedek king of Salem brought out bread and wine; He was the priest of God Most High. And he blessed him and said: "Blessed be Abram of God Most High, Possessor of heaven and earth; and blessed be God Most High, Who has delivered your enemies into your hand."
>
> And he [Abram] gave him a tithe of all.
> (Genesis 14:18-20)

There is no "special secret" to this chapter other than this: If you want to receive God's riches, become a giver. This is what Abram did. He gave ten percent (a tithe) to Melchizedek king of Salem after he came back from routing the enemy who had captured his nephew Lot. When the king of Sodom told Abram to keep the goods he had plundered from Lot's kidnappers for himself, Abram said to the king, "I have raised my hand to the LORD, God Most High, the Possessor of heaven and earth, that I will take nothing, from a thread to a sandal strap, and that I will not take anything that is yours, lest you should say, 'I have made Abram rich....'"

God told Moses some 400 years later that "it is He, the LORD your God...who gives you power to get wealth, that He may establish His covenant which He swore to your fathers, as it is this day." (Deuteronomy 8:18) I believe Abram knew this intuitively and

103

wouldn't allow the king of Sodom to steal the blessing from him, which was the result of his tithing to Melchizedek.

Some religious people get really uptight when you start talking about money and how God will bless you if you give into His kingdom. Immediately, these misguided people start talking about how we shouldn't give to get. I take issue with this philosophy. You can't help but be blessed when you give to the ministry of the Lord. I can speak to this subject with as much or perhaps more credibility than a pastor can because I do not have a non-profit organization that could benefit from your donations. But I will say declaratively and without regret, "If you want to be blessed financially, then you need to give ongoingly to the ministries that are doing the work of the Lord."

I could probably fill an entire book with testimonies of how I have been blessed when I have sewed financial seeds into various ministries and then reaped a financial reward. For the purposes of this chapter, I would like to tell you what happened not too far from where the Rodney King incident took place back in the 1990's.

Our story begins with Julie Dawson, wife of John Dawson, calling me one day to ask about the possibility of listing their house for sale. John is the author of *Taking our Cities for God* and their very neighborhood became the model and example for John's book. He and Julie would take prayer walks and talk with their neighbors on these jaunts. Little by little, they started to see change. When houses would come up for sale, they would pray for the people who would be purchasing and moving into the area. By the time that Julie called, they had seen a marvelous transformation of family after family living in their area with some sort of commitment to God. It was not 100 percent; however, remarkable changes transpired once they began their prayer walks.

When I arrived at the Dawson's home, I learned that John was on a preaching trip somewhere in another part of the country. After giving me a tour of their beautiful house, Julie began her "sales" pitch on me in the living room. Usually it is the other way around. But this time the seller had an idea that she wanted to sell me on. The idea is not one that I especially like because she wanted me to reduce my commission. That happens with a lot more frequency than one might imagine, and I am usually prepared with an answer. However, this time I let her present her case. She wanted a "Big" commission cut—half of what I normally charge for my services. Instead of trying to "sell" her on my marketing plan and why I was worth what I normally charge, I just listened.

When she finished, I told her that the only way I could do what she was asking me to do was if I sold it myself and there was no other cooperating broker involved. Otherwise, I knew of no broker who would want to work for that low of a percentage in a down real estate market. Therefore, I explained that we could not put their house in the MLS and that the buyer would have to come from my marketing efforts exclusively. Since they had a specific time frame that they needed to be moved by, I suggested that if it did not sell in the next 30 days, that we should look at doubling the commission and putting it into the MLS where it would be exposed to thousands of potential buyers. She agreed, and we listed their home with half of my normal commission.

Their house had been added on to and extensively remodeled and upgraded. It was by far the biggest and the best house in the neighborhood. Most of the houses around them were selling for $90,000 less than our asking price. As you can see, I had my work cut out for me—sell an overbuilt house in a time when foreclosures were still a significant force in the Southern California area. Had this home been in a different area, it could have sold for twice what we were asking. Remember the three most important rules for buying real estate? Location, location, location. John and Julie, on the other hand, had bought this house for the same reason (location, location, location), but it was not a financial one. This property was only one block away from a mission organization. John and his parents, Jim and Joy Dawson, have worked with this group for years, so it made sense to buy close by and be able to open their house as part of their ministry to the young missionaries they were training.

No sooner had the ink dried on my listing agreement than a thought came to me about who would be a good candidate to purchase this house. Recently, a young African American couple had left the staff of The Church on the Way to pioneer a new church in the northeast valley. They already lived in the area; however, as the senior pastor of a growing work, it was not too much of a stretch to imagine that they could use a much larger house for ministry purposes.

I got on the phone with the pastor and asked if he and his wife would be interested in looking at this property. When they agreed, we set a time to show them the house. Almost immediately when they walked in, they began to sense that this was a house they could live in for a long, long time and be very happy in. The wife loved the expanded, remodeled kitchen with its dining area and family room close by. The pastor appreciated having a study on the second floor of the house next to the master bedroom. All in all, the house had everything they were looking for—except the right price.

He had already talked to his lender and knew that he only qualified for a loan that was $30,000 less than the Dawson's asking price. We discussed at length what would be the right thing to do. Make an offer? Not make an offer? They didn't want to insult the Dawsons, yet at the same time, they sensed that this might be the house that God would have for them in the next season of their ministry. I assured them that I would present their offer in such a way that it would not hurt the Dawson's feelings—just their pocketbook. (Actually, I didn't say anything about the pocketbook).

When I brought the offer to the Dawson's house, John was again out of town. This time he was in Florida, editing some videotape of a message he had delivered to pastors about racial reconciliation. So in this context, John received my offer to sell his house to a young, black couple who were being called to the 'hood. The only catch was that it was $30,000 less than his asking price. John told me later that as he reviewed the videotape he watched and heard himself say to pastors, "If we want racial reconciliation, we have to be willing to give up things—including the equity in our homes." (*Gulp, "Did I really say that?"* John wondered).

If it had been me in my more immature days, I would definitely have wanted to edit that part out of the videotape. But not John. He knew that he had made the statement and that he would have to live with it. He also knew the character of God and that God would not "rip him off." Having made his decision to accept their offer without countering the price, John called to give me the okay.

The young couple was thrilled to be buying their dream home, yet they still had a hurdle to clear in order to purchase it. They already owned a home that, like virtually every home in Southern California, had gone down in value since they bought it. We figured they had at most $10,000 in equity; however, all of their closing costs in the sale would eat up that money and then some.

Since they didn't yet have the resources to bring cash in to close the sale of their house and buy a new one, they decided to give their house to another couple in their church. This family had been struggling to get going and the pastor's generous gift made it possible for them to establish home ownership without any kind of down payment.

Are you starting to see a pattern evolving here? First I gave up half of my commission. Then John and Julie made the decision to give up $30,000 off the sale of their house. Finally, the African-American couple gave up their entire house, including the right to redeem the husband's VA loan on the house until a later time when the recipients of their generous gift could refinance.

I started off the chapter by saying that the secret to receiving God's riches is to become a giver. When I started the ball rolling by giving half of my commission, God immediately rewarded me with a listing referral from Julie for one of her neighbors. This couple sold their house through me and bought one of my own listings with a full commission. In all, I made back twice what I had given up in commission to the Dawsons. The pastoral couple gave their house away and received another one with almost double the square footage. And when it came time for John and Julie to go find a new home, their REALTOR® in the city where they were moving found a house that they really liked that had been on the market for a long time. She told them that they should not offer their asking price but should come in $30,000 below the listed price. Guess what? The owner took it.

There is a postscript to the Dawson's story. As the closing drew near, it became apparent that the tenant who was living in the house they had purchased was not being cooperative in moving out; therefore, they exercised their right to withdraw and they found another house that equally met their needs and blessed them, as well. Moreover, this time when they purchased, they would be able to benefit financially from having bought in an area that has had high appreciation rates in the past and will probably continue to do so in the future. As I said at the beginning of this chapter, "It is the LORD your God...who gives you power to get wealth that he may establish his covenant." It was my privilege to work with two couples of utmost integrity and see everyone involved with this transaction blessed.

Do not fall into the trap of thinking that they were blessed because they were in the ministry. God's word works for everyone. Like Abram of old, begin to give and start to watch God bless you. There are so many scriptures that support this truth. Some refer to it as the law of sewing and reaping. Just like I said in the chapter on naming ourselves, I speak scriptures out loud all of the time that pertain to my finances. For instance, because I give consistently to my home church and other ministries, I confess according to Luke 6:38, that I give and it is given to me, good measure, pressed down, shaken together and running over do men give unto me. I also confess, "Beloved, I wish above all things that you may prosper and be in good health, even as your soul prospers," (3 John 1:2).

Abraham certainly didn't have a problem with prosperity. The Bible clearly states that he was a wealthy man and everyone knew it. At the end of his life, Abraham sent his servant to find Isaac a wife. Upon meeting the family whose daughter, Rebekah, would become Isaac's wife, the servant told her father, "The LORD has blessed my master abundantly, and he has become wealthy. He has given him sheep and cattle, silver and gold, menservants and maidservants, and camels and donkeys. My master's wife, Sarah, has borne him a son in her old age, and he has given him everything he owns."

A Point of Correction

I would like to address one other issue related to finances in the church. *The Los Angeles Times* recently wrote an article about the fundraising practices of a certain ministry. They quoted one preacher who told the television viewers who were in debt that they needed to give in order to get out of debt. I agree that giving is the pathway to get out of debt. Every day we sew seeds and those seeds will reap a harvest one day. What the preacher said that I do not agree with is that the people who were in debt needed to go further into debt by calling in to the station and putting a donation on their credit card. This is not wise financial guidance.

A person who is in debt does need to give; however, if he does not have ready cash available his giving could be in the form of time donated to a ministry by volunteering two to three hours a week. Every day, millions of people exchange time for money with their employers. They put in forty or more hours and are rewarded with a paycheck at the end of the week. So, without putting their finances in greater jeopardy, people who are in debt could donate their time outside of work to a ministry as a seed they are sewing and expect to see a harvest on that seed—a financial harvest.

The Bible says that seeds produce after their kind, meaning that if you want money, you have to plant money. If you want love, you have to give love. If you want respect, you have to give respect. So, a person without money can still give a financial seed by donating his time. Let's exercise wisdom in our finances and give liberally as the Lord would lead and not as man would lead.

There are preachers on television whom I have the utmost respect for and who would not lead you down the wrong path financially. My spiritual father, Jack Hayford, is one of those people, and he wrote a book called *The Key to Everything*, which explores in detail some of the issues I have just touched on here.

I also have respect for Joyce Meyer and the way she runs her ministry. When Joyce was building her office complex in the late 1990's, she used to publish testimonies from people who had given toward the building project and who had been blessed in their own real estate projects. (Again, seeds produce after their own kind). After reading about this month after month, I felt impressed to plant a seed toward their building, too. The day that I put my check in the mail to Joyce's ministry was the day I signed the contract to buy a fixer-upper house in Woodland Hills, California, a nice suburb in the southwest corner of the San Fernando Valley. Approximately six months later, I flipped the house for a very nice profit.

Some of you more sophisticated readers are probably wondering why I didn't do a 1031 exchange and thereby postpone the real estate taxes indefinitely. You really savvy investors are probably wondering why I didn't keep the house, rent it out and enjoy the phenomenal appreciation that has swept through Southern California in the intervening five years. Today that house is worth more than twice what I sold it for. However, I do not look back. Like Paul, I press toward the mark of the prize of the call of God in Christ Jesus.

I have continued to educate myself about finances, and real estate in particular, and believe that my best years of investing are still ahead of me. One of the paradigm shifts that I have had over the last five years has involved reading virtually all of the books in the *Rich Dad Poor Dad* series. Author Robert Kiyosaki is a strong proponent of developing passive income by having your money work for you instead of you working for money. You can purchase Robert's books at www.RodneyJohnson.com.

You Can't Get Something For Nothing

If you were to ask my wife what one of my favorite pastimes is, she'd immediately tell you that I love to read. One year I read twenty-five books, which ultimately led to a side business of proofreading for a Christian publishing company. I only mention this to set the stage for my next confession. While I have said from the outset of this chapter that giving is the key to receiving and that sewing seeds is the first step in reaping a harvest, you can't get something for nothing.

After the big earthquake in Southern California in 1994, the Lord began dealing with me about giving to every ministry who sent me a solicitation. I made the commitment and started sending in checks to various ministries who contacted us. Some of the checks weren't that large; however, we did send something to them out of obedience. Little by little I started noticing my sales picking up.

At one point, I sold a house that had been repaired after the earthquake for far more than I ever thought it would appraise for. When the appraisal came in without a hitch, I was amazed. While I pondered this sale, the Holy Spirit spoke to me and said, "I gave you this sale because of your giving."

Now that should have been a clue to me to keep doing what He told me to do. Instead, during the course of my insatiable reading, I came across a company who was selling a course in the commodities market whose owner's beliefs were in direct opposition to many of my Christian values. I overlooked the obvious spiritual mismatch and ordered the course. Shortly thereafter, my sales dropped off—dramatically. In fact, I went a couple of months without a single sale.

This, of course, is not good...at all.

When Your Dreams Come Crashing Down

Toward the end of this time, my assistant, Robynn, came in one day and told me about a dream she had the night before. It seems that she had seen me in a restaurant high atop a structure similar to the Seattle Space Needle. In her dream, I was having dinner with an attractive blonde who definitely was not my wife. Robynn approached me and pulled me aside and told me in no uncertain terms that this woman was not going to buy any real estate from me and that I needed to leave immediately. I pooh-poohed her concern and told her there was nothing to worry about. She went to another part of the restaurant and then came back to me later to tell me that if I didn't leave this woman immediately something terribly bad was going to happen. Again, I made light of her observations and ignored her warning. It was then that the restaurant began falling from the sky. Robynn says that she knew she would land safely but she also knew that I was in for a real crash.

When she finished retelling her dream, I assured her that I was NOT having an affair. I did know what the dream was referring to, though. I knew that this course in the commodities I had ordered had been against what I was to be doing with my spare time. Moreover, it was acting like a mistress, in that I was spending too much time on it and my priorities were getting all out of whack. But ultimately, I believe that the underlying spiritual beliefs of the owner were subtly trying to woo me away from my own convictions. When I saw this, I immediately repented, tore up the materials and started back doing what I knew I was called to do.

I want to say here that there is nothing inherently wrong with the commodities market. In fact, my publisher represents a pastor who used to work in the commodities market on Wall Street. My disobedience came from overlooking the prompting I had had about buying the materials in the first place and succumbing to a desire to get something for nothing. Remember, there are no free lunches.

Essentially, I was growing in understanding of a very important key about giving and receiving and allowed myself to get sidetracked by something that had no place in my life. That distraction caused contention within myself, and to some extent with my assistant as well. If I had not repented of my error, I would have likely begun to experience tremendous contention in other areas of my life as well.

In fact, this subject of "contention" leads us into our next chapter. The reality is that it is often "normal" to have some degree of discord and friction when real estate is involved. Consequently, it is important for us to examine this issue in detail to prepare you more fully for your future real estate deals. Continue with me to the next page where we will learn why there is so much contention in so many real estate transactions.

CHAPTER 12

Real Estate Contention

Then Abram went up from Egypt, he and his wife and all that he had, and Lot with him, to the South. Abram was very rich in livestock, in silver, and in gold. Lot also, who went with Abram, had flocks and herds and tents.

Now the land was not able to support them, that they might dwell together, for their possessions were so great that they could not dwell together. And there was strife between the herdsmen of Abram's livestock and the herdsmen of Lot's livestock. So Abram said to Lot, "Please let there be no strife between you and me, and between my herdsmen and your herdsmen; for we are brethren. Is not the whole land before you? Please separate from me. If you take the left, then I will go to the right; or, if you go to the right, then I will go to the left."

And Lot lifted his eyes and saw all the plain of Jordan, that it was well watered everywhere (before the LORD destroyed Sodom and Gomorrah) like the garden of the LORD, like the land of Egypt as you go toward Zoar. Then Lot chose for himself all the plain of Jordan, and Lot journeyed east. And they separated from each other.

And the LORD said to Abram, after Lot had

separated from him: "Lift your eyes now and look from the place where you are--northward, southward, eastward, and westward; for all the land which you see I give to you and your descendants forever. And I will make your descendants as the dust of the earth; so that if a man could number the dust of the earth, then your descendants also could be numbered. Arise, walk in the land through its length and its width, for I give it to you."

(Genesis 13:1-2, 5-7a, 8-11, 14-17)

From this passage we see that Abraham and Lot's servants contended over *land* because there was not enough of it to support each man's livestock. Have you ever wondered why there is so much contention in real estate deals?

When I started selling real estate in 1987, our contract was one legal size page with some "boiler plate" verbiage on the back. Today, the Purchase Agreement in California is eight pages long, with a two-page Buyer's Advisory, plus an agency disclosure. If there is secondary financing, there are another two pages added to the mix. A seller is obligated to give a three-page disclosure statement detailing the inoperative items on the property as well as hazardous substances. If a REALTOR® is involved in the transaction, she is also required to disclose facts materially affecting the value or desirability of the property, as well as give a report on her visual inspection of the house and land. When you add to that an eight page state disclosure, a five-page disclosure from the association of REALTORS®, and all the real estate brokerage firms' disclosures, you have just about leveled a small forest to print all of the paper needed for a real estate transaction! (I hope the reader is beginning to see that a good REALTOR® really earns her commission as she helps sellers provide full disclosure and leads her buyers to make informed purchasing decisions.)

The reason there is so much paperwork is that there have been disputes in the past, and with those disputes come lawsuits. Real estate attorneys are always adding new clauses to the contracts, ostensibly to stem the flow of legal action. For instance, in California there is a

114

time frame for doing inspections, which is typically seventeen days from the date of final acceptance. In the "good ol' days," the method for removing that contingency was the passive method, meaning that if the buyer said nothing then silence was deemed approval on the eighteenth day. Now the method most commonly used to remove contingencies is the active method. This makes it incumbent upon the seller to put in writing his request for the buyer to lift his contingencies. If the buyer refuses to do so, then the seller may cancel the agreement; however, he cannot keep the buyer's deposit in most circumstances.

As you can see, there are a myriad of things to keep straight in a real estate transaction and, when they are not kept entirely to the letter of the law, often because people's personalities get in the way, contention can arise.

It amazes me that some people come in with an entirely skeptical, contrarian attitude. It seems as if they are looking to pick a fight and that somebody needs to win and somebody needs to lose in the typical deal. I do not like dealing with people who behave in this manner. However, somewhere along the line, be it either with the buyer, seller, agents, or other affiliated personnel like escrow officers, loan agents, title reps, or inspectors, someone feels the need to flex their muscles and make threats or "contend" with another party. When that happens, my job becomes one of referee or arbitrator—and not one that I particularly enjoy.

Joyce Meyer is a preacher whose cassettes and CDs find themselves in my car on any number of occasions. I enjoy listening to her wit and wisdom during my travels. She has a teaching entitled, "New Level, New Devil" that essentially says that anytime we move up in responsibilities and leadership in God's kingdom we will encounter a new demonic attack that will endeavor to keep us from fulfilling our purpose in this new realm of influence. I agree with her assessment because I see it all of the time in my line of work as a real estate broker. Abraham experienced it, too, as he was trying to fulfill God's call to go to a new land. His contention came from his relative, Lot, and his herdsmen.

Many times, relatives will seek to keep one of their own from fulfilling their destiny as it relates to real estate ownership. They may not intend to do so, but their negativity and words of doubt play right into the enemy's hands in keeping their "kin folk" right where they have always been. (For more information, see Joyce's website at www.joycemeyer.org where you will find information on how to get this fine teaching.)

Doo-Wap Ditty

Speaking of Joyce, another of her teachings helped me as I was contending with a celebrity client I will refer to as "Doo-Wap Ditty" or "DWD" for short. This entertainer had been the featured guest one year at the Century 21 convention and happened to mention from the stage that the DWD family wanted to move back to Southern California. While REALTORS® were throwing their business cards on the platform to solicit his business, I slipped out of the convention arena and called a friend who worked for DWD. I told him what his employer had said and wondered if he could make the connection for me to show DWD property. He agreed, and in a matter of a few days, I was on the phone learning the needs and wants of the DWD clan.

When they arrived in town, I had several houses lined up to show them, but nothing really piqued their interest. When I showed them a new house, they really perked up. However, in time, their business manager put the "kibosh" on spending over a million dollars.

When DWD would come to town, he expected me to drop whatever I was doing and show him and his family property on as little as 30 minute's notice. After we had been looking for several months, I introduced them to a new development in the Southwest corner of the San Fernando Valley. Finally, I had hit on something that they liked. I registered DWD with the new home builder and proceeded to bring the paperwork over to the studio where this entertainer was recording.

During the initial phase of registering my client, DWD's true colors were exposed when an argument broke out with builder's salesperson. I couldn't believe that someone who wanted to live in this development would talk to a salesperson in such a condescending tone of voice. After I got to the studio with the paperwork, DWD decided that the family was not ready to make a financial commitment. Months had already passed working with this mini-tyrant, and now it was coming to no avail.

Every so often I would get a call from DWD but a year passed without a purchase. Then I heard through the grapevine that DWD had bought a house in the very development I had first shown the family.

The Bible says that the workman is worthy of his hire—meaning you should be paid for your services—so I called the builder direct to ask for my commission, which was in excess of $20,000. He confirmed that DWD had indeed bought a house from him. In fact, he remembered I had registered my client because of the big fuss made with his sales associate. So when DWD tried to circumvent me, the builder pulled my registration, only to learn that the six-month time period had elapsed and that this singer could legally buy without my assistance. He chose to do the dishonorable thing, and I was out approximately $20,000.

On one of my treks around town, I was listening to another teaching tape from Joyce Meyer about forgiving those who have wronged us. She said that lack of forgiveness allows strife into our lives and that is one thing I did not need. So, as I pulled into my parking lot, I made a commitment to forgive DWD for not acting with integrity toward me and cutting me out of a significant commission.

Right about this time, I was representing a couple who were selling a house in the same city where DWD lived. We had an offer to purchase their house just as my listing was canceling. However, it was so low that our counter offer didn't even make a blip on the buyer's radar screen. It seemed that the deal was dead and that I had lost a second very large sale. Within hours after making a decision to forgive DWD, I learned that the buyer's agent wanted to know if my sellers would accept a counter proposal. I called them with the offer and they agreed to the countered price, as their circumstances had changed since I first listed and subsequently canceled their house.

On the heels of my forgiving DWD, I received a counter offer for a transaction that was as good as dead. Coincidence? You be the judge. Me? I believe that the buyer's agent would never have called had I not chosen to forgive the person who wronged me. Moreover, the price for the salvaged deal was almost the same as the one I was cut out of by DWD.

New Level, New Devil

In 1999, I sensed that I was to begin developing a clientele in the upper price echelons of Southern California realty, particularly in the San Fernando Valley where my office was located. What did Joyce say? "New level, new devil." The first listing that I took for just under $1 million in a gated community in Chatsworth soon verified her premise. My advertising generated a call from a single woman I will call the "Three Hundred Million Dollar Trust Baby" or "3TB" for short. Suffice it to say that even though she showed financial statements purporting to be worth in excess of $300,000,000, she could not or would not release a $30,000 deposit check for the property. This woman played on the emotions of the seller, the lender, an attorney, the escrow officer, and me.

Right on the heels of ridding myself of 3TB, a couple was referred to me who wanted to buy a 10,000 square foot home in the northwest area of the San Fernando Valley. The man presented himself as a former professional football player from the Canadian league and was now doing commercial development in a northern state. Like 3TB, he showed me photos of a marina he had ostensibly built. He drove a Cadillac Escalade and lived in a hotel, so he seemed motivated to purchase and close. They had previously been in escrow on a mansion in one of the gated communities but did not close on it. Like 3TB, this client manipulated my time, and an architect's time, and not to mention the seller or listing agent's time. Ultimately, he ended up in jail for stealing his ex-wife's Escalade and leaving the state.

So what does a person of faith do when facing new obstacles at a new level? What did Abraham do? You'll note that he did not get into strife with his nephew. In fact, he let Lot choose what seemed to be the choicest parcel of land without even a hint of contesting his decision. As kingdom people, we are admonished to be "wise as serpents and harmless as doves." I take that to mean that we

118

recognize that our struggle is not with people. As the Apostle Paul says, "We wrestle not against flesh and blood but against powers, principalities, and spiritual wickedness in high places."

With two high ticket deals sabotaged by counterfeit buyers with hidden agendas, I recognized that I was in a struggle and that my struggle was not with either of these two. The word says that in the multitude of counselors there is safety. Typically, when situations arise like the ones I have just described, I have men in my life that I go to for wise counsel.

Two men in particular had been privy to the details of these deals; however, I sensed that I needed to talk to a pastor. Normally, I would have called our then-senior pastor, Scott Bauer, and asked to see him for breakfast or lunch. This time, though, I felt prompted to send a note to the man I call my spiritual father, Jack Hayford, and see if he had time in his busy schedule. Not long after sending him my letter, I was asked to lead worship for a group of preachers that Pastor Jack was speaking to. At that meeting, he indicated that he was available the very next morning for breakfast.

Seated in a booth at the back of the International House of Pancakes (IHOP), I opened our discussion by telling him about my sensing a call to develop my business in the high end of real estate while maintaining my clientele in the mid-level prices. The obstacles encountered with these two buyers were an integral part of setting the stage. In short order, we both recognized that this was a matter requiring prayer. Right there in IHOP we bowed our heads and began to pray. Pastor Jack prayed with a fervor that I have not seen before or since in a restaurant. As we got up to leave, he reached for his billfold and handed me $2.10. He said that he felt prompted to give that to me as a down payment on the $2.1 million sale that had been stolen from me by the "Faux Football Player" (or "FFP" for short).

I did not immediately run right out and sell another $2.1 million house; however, within the next 30 days I made what would have amounted to a $1.25 million dollar sale by combining three or four deals that happened on the heels of our meeting and prayer time at IHOP. In the intervening time, I have sold two estates priced in the $2.1 million dollar range. Like Abraham with Lot, I didn't have to go after the person who was the source of the contention. With Pastor

Jack's help, I went after the real adversary in prayer and defeated him–and just left the other two in God's very capable hands.

If you are encountering obstacles in your real estate endeavors, recognize like Abraham did, that people are not your enemies. Instead, seek Godly counsel. Prayer is the key to moving forward in your plan of attack.

After Lot moved away from Abram, the Lord told Abram to lift up his eyes toward the land. Every piece of land that he saw was to be his. However, he was also told to walk the length and breadth of it. There will be times when we have to do something physical to break a spiritual stronghold over the land just like I did in the story I told you in chapter one about Mitch and Tracy, and the clapping of hands.

Untying a Very Large Knot

The first time I realized this was when I was listing and selling the foreclosures for Bank of America. I had been given a beautiful custom home in a gated community. The house had over 6,500 square feet of living space and had been built by the owner who was foreclosed on. After I was given the listing by the bank, I had several offers on it but nothing was coming together. One day driving in to work, my assistant, Robynn Creitz, was praying for our listings. When she came to this particular bank-owned property, the Holy Spirit whispered to her spirit, *This house is tied up in knots.* She told me about her experience when she got in to work.

We both felt that someone needed to go to the property and pray through the house, untying as it were, the spiritual knots that were keeping this house from selling. I recognized immediately that the negative things that I had been hearing from agents showing the house were becoming a curse to the property. Also, I could just imagine the owner/builder being evicted and shouting things such as, "You'll never sell or if you do, it will be for such a low price that the bank would have been better off never having taken it back." No wonder it was "tied up in knots."

Robynn and I decided to go to the house together and pray through it, asking God's blessing on it and for Him to bring a buyer who would be blessed by owning such a magnificent home. After we had prayed through each room, we ended up on the front door step and literally acted as though we were untying a knot. That may sound silly; however, God's order to the Israelites to march around Jericho seven times without saying a word probably sounded silly too.

When He told them to shout, the walls came down. I do not recall being prompted to shout. But I did declare forthrightly that as a child of the Most High God, I had the right to rule and reign over this vacant property while I was being entrusted with its listing. And with that right, I was untying any knots that had come into being due to the words that had been spoken negatively over this property. Within a week, the house sold and closed in short order. In fact, the buyer was the couple I was meeting with when I received the call from Garrett that Mitch and Tracy's house had closed!

It is no coincidence that Paul told the early Christians to "fight the good fight." Just remember that people are not our enemies. The DWD, the 3TB, and FFP were not my enemies even though it seemed like it at the time. A setback or contention encountered may actually mean that you are on the right path! Seek out counsel and proceed prayerfully to gain the victory. Then, as the next chapter will explain, just "throw your hat on the other side of the fence" and go for it!

CHAPTER 13

Throw Your Hat on the Other Side of the Fence

Imagine a group of adolescent boys who have gotten together to spend the day out in the meadows of Ireland. With nothing to do except explore the wonders around them, they set off, full of energy and excitement. One calls out, "Race you to the rock wall," which was more than a hundred yards away. Off they ran, sprinting like a would-be Jesse Owens or Carl Lewis. Out of breath, they arrived at the huge rock wall only to see it menacingly towering over them. It was wide, too. In fact, they couldn't see where it started or stopped. If someone didn't come up with a plan fairly quickly, their adventure was about to be over almost before it started.

Without a word, the leader took off his precious cap and hurled it high in the air. Up it sailed and over to the other side of the fence. The other boys in the group stared at the leader incredulously. "What are you thinking?" one of them asked. "That was your best hat," another volunteered. "Your mom will kill you if you don't come home with that cap," a third lamented. "Not only am I going to get my cap, I will race you to the next wall, too," the leader challenged. Not to be outdone, all of the young boys began throwing their hats over the fence. For a moment they looked at each other, secretly thinking, "Why did I just do something as stupid as that?"

The leader moved down the wall, touching the rocks as he went. In short order, he found a rock that was loose. "Hey, come here," he hollered. Within moments they were all pulling rocks out of the wall and in no time flat, they had an opening big enough to climb through. You have never seen such relief as they all retrieved their prized possessions—their hats.

So, it continued for the rest of the day. They would race to another wall and throw their hats on the other side of the fence. Sometimes they couldn't find a way to make an opening, so they'd boost each other up to scale the wall. One time they had to walk the entire length and go around the wall. By the time they got back to their hats, they appreciated them all the more. At day's end, they each returned home realizing that they were capable of doing more than they had ever imagined.

A Guidepost for Living

I read a piece in *Guideposts* magazine about a man who had heard of this same Irish custom that I illustrated in the previous story, and used it as motivation to make his way as a young man in Chicago. With permission from the editors at *Guideposts,* I turned his story into a song. The lyrics are as follows:

A fishing boat named Dixie was my father's pride and joy
And Dad left home in Dixie while still a teenaged boy
The Windy City called his name to make his way down there
But times were tough and jobs were scarce and things weren't always fair
It would have been so easy to turn his boat around
And head back for the safety of that small Wisconsin town

    So when you come to a wall that's too hard to climb
    When you're down to your last nickel and you're running out of time
    When you're tempted to give up
    When things ain't makin' sense
    Take your hat off and throw it on the other side of the fence

I asked him what he meant; why should I waste a hat
But he said, "Listen closely, son, it means much more than that
I loved that boat named Dixie. She brought me to my dream.
But if I kept her on the bank she could take me upstream.
I didn't want to go home, so I sold her for the rent.

And that's how I threw my hat on the other side of the fence."

So when you come to a wall that's too hard to climb
When you're down to your last nickel and you're running
out of time
When you're tempted to give up
When things ain't makin' sense
Take your hat off and throw it on the other side of the fence

You'll find a way to get around it
You'll find a way to scale that wall
You might have to fly right over it
Like a human cannon ball

So when you come to a wall that's too hard to climb
When you're down to your last nickel and you're running
out of time
When you're tempted to give up
When things ain't makin' sense
Take your hat off and throw it on the other side of the fence

Refreshing Music ©1996

In many ways, Abraham's story, my story and your story, parallel the events of this song. Abraham received a call to come out of his father's house and come to a land that God would show him. If that is not an example of throwing your hat on the other side of the fence, I don't know what is.

On January 1, 1981, I said goodbye to my parents and watched them drive off, leaving me in Los Angeles all alone with just a few dollars in my bank account and virtually no contacts. Still, I was not about to turn around and follow them home until I had captured my hat on the other side of the fence—literally on the other side of the country. Throughout my career, I have had to throw my hat on the other side of the fence time and again when I was attempting to do something new or different. When I had no money, hiring an assistant to help me go after the foreclosure market was certainly an example of throwing my hat on the other side of the fence.

If you picked up this book expecting to learn something about real estate, I hope that you have been challenged to throw your hat on the other side of the fence, too. For some, that may mean purchasing a course on real estate to further your knowledge. Others may already have the knowledge but haven't had the mindset that they could do it.

To them I say, "What are you waiting for?" You were destined for greatness, so stop procrastinating. Take your hat off and throw it on the other side of the fence!

Your first step could be to put down this book in a few moments and immediately call a REALTOR®. For others, your action point could be to pick up a newspaper and start calling owners whose houses are for sale. Even in hot real estate markets, there are good deals to be found. Be persistent. Have faith that you are being led to the right property.

Others may want to hop on the internet and visit my website at www.RodneyJohnson.com to learn what the next step is for them. There is a world of excitement for you out there if you will take your hat off and throw it on the other side of the fence.

Conclusion

I once got into a discussion with a woman about the scripture that says,

"Eye has not seen, nor ear heard; neither has it entered into the hearts of man the things God has prepared for us."

(1 Corinthians 2:9)

She stopped there in her quotation of that verse...and was quite surprised when I pointed out that the Apostle Paul quoted that passage from the Old Testament (Isaiah 64:4) and then went on to say:

"But God has revealed them to us by His Spirit."

(1 Corinthians 2:10)

You do not have to wait until you get to heaven to get your Promised Land. God will reveal by His Spirit the steps you are to take to possess yours. I encourage you to believe that God will put his "super" on your "natural" and make you supernaturally gifted to superintend the properties He has for you. If you will live in the knowledge that God wants you to exercise dominion over the land while you are living on this earth, He'll give you a picture of your dream. Ask Him to help you develop a great team of people who will help you achieve your collective goals. You can speak to your dream and give it a name. You can sign your name to the title deed of that dream and live free of fear while pursuing it. You can trust God to bring it about and bring the right people into your path to make it come to pass. More importantly, you can give your way to getting everything that you want and you can win even when people and things are contending with you.

Start now. Abraham did it and he was not the least bit prepared when he received his call. You can do it too. Take your hat off and one, two, three…throw!

—Not "The End," but just the beginning—

POSSESSING *YOUR*
PROMISED LAND

Resources
to help you
Possess Your Promised Land

www.RodneyJohnson.com
Your comprehensive real estate web site!

In addition to providing you convenient links to the books referenced within *Possessing Your Promised Land: Biblical Principles for Real Estate Acquisition*, you can also:

- Access Rodney's professional real estate listings.

- Find contact information on how to be coached by Rodney—whether you are a real estate professional or a consumer wishing to purchase your own properties.

- Obtain information on how to book Rodney to speak at your church or event.

- Sign up for Rodney's new internet reality television show—*Insider Real Estate TV*.

- Access *My Real Estate Blueprint,* Rodney's real estate blog, to read his latest postings—and even ask Rodney your questions!

- Take Rodney's e-mail course—"21 Days to a Changed Mindset."

- And more!

Also, be sure to download the latest TRINSPIRATION™ Sampler for your personal enrichment, as was featured earlier in this book.

With all the resources available to you there, you will surely want to visit this site again and again. So, be sure to bookmark www.RodneyJohnson.com into your web browser's "favorites" list for future ease of access. Furthermore, please feel free to tell all your friends about this unique Christian real estate resource on the Web!

—The Publisher

BargainChristianBooks.com

An outstanding online Christian bookstore and more! This phenomenal site offers over 150,000 books, gift items, homeschool supplies, music, software and more—with most items 20% or more off the suggested retail price everyday. Even more exciting is the huge selection of family-friendly and Christian videos!

BargainChristianBooks.com also has services links to additional resources and products through other Christian providers. Without question, this site truly offers believers excellent value when seeking "bargains" or doing their shopping online. Visit them today!

ProVisionNetwork.org

A growing international network of Christian business owners and professionals that is advancing the Kingdom! Founded by Wall Street Millionaire and Christian pastor, Dan Stratton, this organization seeks to network those who have business and professional callings with each other to help propagate the gospel by increasing the financial resources of Christ's Church.

Their web site includes Dan's phenomenal biography, details about the network, and links to many Christian resources and businesses. Whether you are a minister, professional, business owner or consumer—there are plenty of things on this site to bless you. Check them out today!

ThriftyGetaway.com

Airline tickets, hotels, car rental, vacation and cruise packages—at prices lower than most of their secular online competitors! You should consider shopping ThriftyGetaway.com before buying from any non-Christian site. Why? You are not only supporting the business of another believer, but saving money to boot!

The entrance page (which you should bookmark) even offers you an opportunity to learn how to become a freelance travel agent and save even more—plus get special perodic "agent only" travel incentives!

Be sure to visit ThriftyGetaway.com and book your future travel arrangements for less!

(Note: Be sure to remember that there is no "s" on the end of "getaway" if you want to be sure and find the Christian URL, and not one of its secular competitors.)

Featured new release:

Paradigm ™
Seed Publishers, Inc.

ISBNs:

1-033141-00-X
("hardback")

1-933141-01-8
("paperback")

1-933141-02-6
(e-Book edition)

What do you get when...

You combine a Wall Street millionaire, Christian pastor, and a Hebrew scholar? Answer: **Dan Stratton**

"...I have seen His anointing in the markets of New York as a trader and as a pastor. After many years of learning the world's system—and now His system in the world—I have come to know that there is a real contest being waged, and only the prepared man or woman will get the spoils. He who wields his faith with wisdom and with boldness will take his rightful place in His plan. I have been called to find such men and women and help them to position themselves for the greatest move of God that the earth has ever seen." —**Excerpt from Divine ProVision**

Available November 2005 everywhere!

You can save money *online* by ordering it <u>today</u> on
BargainChristianBooks.com

GLOSSARY OF REAL ESTATE TERMS

The following *Glossary of Real Estate Terms* is provided for the purpose of expanding your comprehension of the industry terminology, as well as to help you with any specific words that you may be unfamiliar with that occur within the text of this book. However, there are a few caveats you need to keep in mind as you read these terms:

1. Although most of them are common to the industry throughout the United States, some may not be used in professional practice in every locality. We also may have omitted a few that are used only in special circumstances, or rarely in most states.

2. Even when these same terms are in use, there can be varying shades of meaning (i.e., different definitions) depending on your locality. Where possible, we have attempted to note known U.S. variations in defining a term. However, it is possible that we missed a few while compiling this resource.

With those two warnings in mind, I want to once more encourage you to always employ the services of a qualified real estate and/or legal professional in your geographic area. Such expert assistance will ensure that you have the right information for your specific circumstances. Again, these definitions are provided as a reference tool only, and are not to be construed as specific legal or professional advice applicable to your particular situation.

Common Real Estate Terms

Accession – Acquisition of property by its incorporation with other property.

Acre – One acre equals 43,560 square feet.

Ad Valorem – According to value.

Adverse Possession – A means of acquiring property based on continued use and payment of taxes.

Amortization – To liquidate or to extinguish an obligation on an installment basis.

Appraisal – The estimated present worth of the property.

Attachment Lien – An involuntary specific lien against property that terminates in three years.

Avulsion – Sudden violent action that results in the loss of a portion of land.

Balloon Payment Loan – A loan that has been only partially amortized and where there will be a balance still due and owing on the loan at its maturity.

Beneficiary – The lender in a transaction.

Bill of Sale – Transfers personal property and requires signature of the seller.

Blanket Mortgage or Trust Deed – A mortgage or trust deed which covers more than one lot or parcel or real property; it often covers an entire subdivision. As individual lots are sold, a partial reconveyance from the blanket mortgage is ordinarily obtained.

Boot – Dissimilar property, such as money, given as part of the consideration in the exchange of properties having different values. Boot compensates for difference in value.

Capitalization Rates – The return on (such as interest) and the return of (depreciation recaptured) the investment.

Chattel – Personal property.

Chain of Title – A continuous history of all conveyances and encumbrances against a piece of property from the earliest record to the present.

Cloud on Title – A claim on property title which impairs the owner's ability to transfer the property. It can be removed only if the claim is satisfied, or a court with jurisdiction makes an action against it. In some localities, it can refer only to an *invalid* encumbrance on real property and not to encumbrances in general—as it is in most localities.

Collateral – Any property pledged as security for a debt, e.g., the real estate pledged as security for a mortgage or deed of trust.

Community Property – property owned only by husband and wife and where there is a presumption of such title unless specified in writing to the contrary.

Condominium – Ownership of a divided interest, i.e., an individually owned unit, in a multifamily or other structure, together with an undivided interest in common areas.

Conservator – A person appointed by the probate court to take care of the person or property of an adult person needing such care.

Consideration – The inducement for entering into a contract; it consists of either a benefit to the promisor, or a loss or detriment to the promisee.

Constructive Notice – Notice given by the public records of a claim of ownership or interest in property.

Contiguous – Being in actual contact; touching.

Contingent – Dependent upon an uncertain future event.

Contract – An agreement by which a person undertakes to do or not to do a certain thing.

Contract Rent – Refers to the actual lease amount of a unit and could be above or below market rate (economic rent).

Conventional Loan – A mortgage loan which is not insured or guaranteed by a governmental agency.

Conveyance – A written instrument transferring the title to land or an interest therein from one person to another.

Covenants – Agreements contained in deeds and other instruments for the performance or nonperformance of certain acts, or the use or nonuse of property in a certain manner.

Cul-de-sac – Refers to a dead end street that is wider at the end to allow for turns.

Declaration of Homestead – Document recorded by a homeowner to protect his home from a forced sale up to a prescribed amount in satisfaction of certain types of creditors.

Deed – Written instrument by which the ownership of land is transferred from one person to another.

Deed of Trust – A security device that secures the promissory note and contains many protective clauses for the lender.

Default – Failure to perform a duty or to discharge an obligation.

Deficiency Judgment – A personal judgment in foreclosure action for the amount remaining due after a sale of the security.

Demography – The study of the population.

Deposit Receipt – Used when accepting "earnest money" to bind an offer for property by a prospective purchaser; also includes terms of a contract.

Depreciation – The loss of property value from any cause.

Devise – A gift of real property by will.

Devisee – One who receives real property by will.

Domicile – A person's legal residence.

Due-on-sale Clause – A provision in a real estate loan calling for automatic maturity at the lender's option on a sale or transfer of the real property to a third party. Also called alienation clause.

Earnest Money – Something given as a part of the purchase price to bind a bargain.

Easement – A right or interest in the land of another existing apart from the ownership of the land, such as a right to cross over another person's property.

Economic Life – The productive life of the property.

Economic Rent – Refers to the going "market rate" for rent of a given unit, and is used for the appraisal of income property.

Effective Age – Refers to the condition of the property, and is used in the appraisal report.

Eminent Domain – The right or power of the government to take property for a public purpose upon payment of just compensation.

Encroachment – The extension of an improvement onto the property of another.

Encumbrance – Anything that burdens, limits or affects the title on a property.

Equity – The difference between what is owed against the property and what it could sell for.

Escheat – The reverting of property to the state in cases where the owner dies intestate and without heirs.

Escrow – A neutral third party between a buyer and seller to carry out the directions of said parties.

Estate for Life – An estate held by a person to continue during his life or for the life of any other designated person.

Estate for Years – An interest in land based on a contract for the possession of land by a tenant or lessee for a definite or fixed period of time. The period can be either more or less than a year.

Estate of Inheritance – An estate which may descend to heirs. A fee simple estate is an estate of inheritance.

Executor – A person who is designated in a will as the representative of a decedent's estate.

Federal Housing Administration (FHA) – A federal agency, created by the National Housing Act of 1934, for the purpose of expanding and strengthening home ownership by making private mortgage financing possible on a long term, low-down payment basis.

Fee – An estate of inheritance.

Fee Appraiser – A person who is self-employed and charges a fee for each appraisal report.

Fee Simple – The greatest interest one can have in the land.

Fee Simple Absolute – An estate in real property which gives the

139

owner the greatest power over the title. It establishes the title or real property in the owner without limitation.

Foreclosure – A proceeding to enforce a lien by a sale of the property in order to satisfy the debt.

Fully Amortized Loan – A loan that is reduced to nothing by a series of equal installment payments over a given period of time.

Functional Obsolescence – Features that are outdated on a property that can cause it to lose value, compared to other properties.

Grant – Transfer of real property.

Grant Deed – Transfers title and must be signed by the grantor.

Grantee – The person to whom a grant is made or the buyer.

Grantor – The person who makes the grant or the seller.

Ground Lease – A lease covering the land only and not the improvements which are to be installed by the lessee.

HUD – Stands for "Housing and Urban Development"; the government agency that handles all matters of fair housing.

Impound Account – An account set up to pay taxes and insurance as they come due.

Installment Note – A promissory note providing for payment of the principal in two or more certain amounts at different stated times.

Instrument – A writing, such as a deed, made and executed as the expression of some act, contract, or proceeding.

Interest – The proprietary right or share in, ownership of, financial or legal claim to, any real property.

Intestate – Having made no will. A decedent who has left no will is said to have "died intestate."

Joint Tenancy – Title held by two or more persons in equal shares with right of survivorship.

Junior Lien – A subordinate lien.

Land Sales Contract – A contract used in connection with the sale of real property where the seller retains legal title until all or a certain part of the purchase price is paid by the buyer. Often used when property is sold on a small down payment.

Lease – A possessory interest in the property of another for a definite period of time, without transferring title.

Lessee – The tenant under a lease.

Lessor – The landlord under a lease.

Leverage – The ability of the borrower to control a large investment with a relatively small amount of his or her own money.

Lien – A money encumbrance, which can include loans and taxes.

Life Estate – An estate measured by the life of a natural person.

Liquidated Damages – An agreed to sum of money to be paid under a contract in the event of a breach where it would be difficult to prove the amount of actual damages.

Lis Pendens – A notice of the filing of an action; a pending lawsuit usually regarding the title to real property that becomes effective when it is filed.

Listing – An employment contract between a broker and his client.

Location – The most important factor influencing the value of a property.

Novation – The substitution of a new contract for an old one by the mutual agreement of the parties.

Marketable Title – A title free from reasonable doubt in law and in fact.

Market Value – The price that property would reasonably be expected to bring if it were offered for sale with a reasonable sales effort over a reasonable period.

Mortgage – A written document executed by the owner of land by which the land is given as security for the payment of a debt or performance of an obligation.

Mortgage Banker – A company or individual engaged in the business of originating mortgage loans with its own funds, selling those loans to long-term investors, and servicing the loans for the investor until they are paid in full.

Mortgagee – The party who obtains the benefit of a mortgage.

Mortgagor – The party who executes a mortgage.

Multiple Listing – An organized real estate listing service under which brokers pool their listings.

Note – A written acknowledgment of a debt by a borrower including a promise of payment in accordance with specified terms; an evidence of debt; the credit instrument. Also referred to as a promissory note.

Notice of Default – Recorded notice that a default has occurred under a deed of trust.

Notice to Quit – Notice to a tenant to vacate.

Option – A right to require an act to be done in the future.

Oral Contract – One not in writing.

Ownership – The right to the use and enjoyment of property to the exclusion of others.

Percentage Lease – Usually based on a percentage of monthly gross income.

Personal Property – Moveable property such as cars, furniture, clothing, etc.

Power of Attorney – A written authorization to an agent to perform specified acts on behalf of his principal. May be a general power or a limited power.

Prepayment Penalty – Lump sum payment of interest to the lender by the borrower for the privilege of being released from the contract, which calls for long term payments.

Principal – One who employs an agent to act on his behalf.

Probate Court – The branch of the Superior Court that administers the estates of decedents, incompetents, minors, missing persons and so on.

Procuring Cause – The cause of originating a series of events that leads to the consumption (completion) of a sale. Applies primarily to real estate brokers in most localities.

Promissory Note – Evidence of the debt containing the promise to pay, the signature of the borrower and must be secured by another device, usually the trust deed.

Promotional Note – A short term note of up to and including 36 months in its term

Property – The rights or interest that a person has in the thing owned.

Property Taxes – Calculated on a certain percentage of assessed value of a property.

Prorate – To divide equally or proportionately to the time of use. In a sales escrow, it is the custom to prorate taxes, interest, rents, and hazard insurance premiums between buyer and seller in accordance with the respective periods of ownership.

Purchase Money Deed of Trust – A deed of trust to secure payment of all or a portion of the purchase price of real property.

Quiet Title – An action to establish title to real property.

Quitclaim Deed – A deed which conveys whatever present right, title or interest the grantor may have.

Real Property – Land and buildings affixed to the land, including the air space above and the mineral rights below.

Reconveyance – A conveyance to the land owner of the title held by a trustee under a deed of trust.

Recordation – Filing for the record in the office of the county recorder.

Rent – The consideration for the use of a property, and is legally due at the end of a term.

Request for Notice of Default – A notice recorded on behalf of the holder of a junior lien requesting that he be notified in the event that a notice of default is recorded under a prior deed of trust.

Riparian Rights – Water rights, or rights by a watercourse such as a stream or river.

Sales Tax – The tax on tangible personal property only.

Seasoned Note – A note that is 36 months and one day or longer in its term.

Sheriff's Deed – Deed given to the purchaser at an execution sale of real property after the redemption period has expired.

Sublease – Transfers possession of the property from the original tenant to another tenant.

Spouse – A husband or wife.

Tax Deed – A deed issued to the purchaser at a tax sale.

Tenancy in Common – Ownership of property by two or more persons in an undivided interest without right of survivorship.

Tender – An unconditional offer of payment of a debt.

Testate – Having made a will. A decedent who made a will is said to have "died testate."

Title – Evidence of a person's right or the extent of his or her interest in property.

Township – A six-mile square, containing 36 square miles, with a 24-mile perimeter.

Triple-net Lease – A lease wherein the tenant pays a net amount plus all property taxes, insurance and maintenance of the property.

Trust – A fiduciary relationship in which one party (trustee) holds the title to property for the benefit of another party (beneficiary).

Trust Deed – Same as deed of trust.

Trustee – The person to whom property is conveyed in trust or the one who holds title to property as trustee under the terms of a deed of trust.

Trustee's Deed – Deed given by the trustee under a deed of trust when the property is sold under the power of sale.

Trustor – Under a trust deed, the trustor is the person who conveys property in trust or the borrower and the party who signs the note and the deed of trust itself.

Unlawful Detainer – The legal action an owner can take for removal of a defaulting tenant.

Usury – Taking more interest than the law allows on a loan; charging an illegal rate or amount of interest on a loan.

Vendee – Purchaser.

Vendor – Seller.

Veterans Administration – An independent agency of the federal government created by the Serviceman's Readjustment Act of 1944 to administer a variety of benefit programs designated to facilitate the adjustment of returning veterans to civilian life. Among the benefit programs is the Home Loan Guaranty program designed to encourage mortgage lenders to offer long-term low down payment financing to eligible veterans by guaranteeing the lender against loss on these higher risk loans.

Void – Having no legal effect; null.

Voidable – An instrument that appears to be valid, but is in fact lacking in some essential requirement.

Warranty – An assurance or undertaking that certain defects do not exist.

Writ – A process of the court under which property may be seized and sold.

Writ of Execution – A court order that forces the sale of property to pay off a judgment.

Zoning – Governmental regulations relating to the use of real property.

Scriptures for
Possessing Your Promised Land™

As you read the following scriptures, take note of the many references to houses, land, building, doors and windows. Is it a coincidence that Jesus was a carpenter? I think not. It is obvious that God cares about every detail of our lives, down to the design of our house. May your faith increase to believe God for homes and lands to rule and reign over in *this* life.

The greatest homes and lands are yet to come in our *Heavenly* estate! I want to see you there, too.

HOUSE

Genesis 12:1
Now the LORD had said to Abram: "Get out of your country, from your family and from your father's **house**, to a land that I will show you."

Genesis 18:19
For I have known him, in order that he may command his children and his **household** after him, that they keep the way of the LORD, to do righteousness and justice, that the LORD may bring to Abraham what He has spoken to him.

Deuteronomy 6:7
You shall teach them diligently to your children, and shall talk of them when you sit in your **house**, when you walk by the way, when you lie down, and when you rise up.

Deuteronomy 26:11
So you shall rejoice in every good thing which the LORD your God has given to you and your **house**....

Deuteronomy 28:8
The LORD will command the blessing on you in your storehouses and in all to which you set your hand, and He will bless you in the land which the LORD your God is giving you.

Joshua 24:15
But as for me and my **house**, we will serve the LORD.

I Samuel 2:35
Then I will raise up for Myself a faithful priest who shall do according to what is in My heart and in My mind. I will build him a sure **house**, and he shall walk before My anointed forever.

I Samuel 25:6
And thus you shall say to him who lives in prosperity: "Peace be to you, peace to your **house**, and peace to all that you have!"

I Chronicles 17:10
Furthermore, I tell you that the LORD will build you a **house**.

Ezra 3:11
Then all the people shouted with a great shout, when they praised the LORD, because the foundation of the **house** of the LORD was laid.

Job 1:10
Have You not made a hedge around him, around his **household**, and around all that he has on every side? You have blessed the work of his hands, and his possessions have increased in the land.

Job 21:9
Their **houses** are safe from fear, neither is the rod of God upon them.

Job 22:18
He filled their **houses** with good things; but the counsel of the wicked is far from me.

Psalm 49:16
Do not be afraid when one becomes rich, when the glory of his **house** is increased.

Psalm 127:1
Unless the LORD builds the **house**, they labor in vain who build it; unless the LORD guards the city, the watchman stays awake in vain.

Psalm 128:3
Your wife shall be like a fruitful vine in the very heart of your **house**, your children like olive plants all around your table.

Proverbs 12:7
The wicked are overthrown and are no more, but the **house** of the righteous will stand.

Proverbs 14:1
The wise woman builds her **house**, but the foolish pulls it down with her hands.

Proverbs 15:6
In the **house** of the righteous there is much treasure, but in the revenue of the wicked is trouble.

Proverbs 24:3
Through wisdom a **house** is built, and by understanding it is established.

Matthew 7:25
...and the rain descended, the floods came, and the winds blew and beat on that **house**; and it did not fall, for it was founded on the rock.

Mark 3:25
And if a **house** is divided against itself, that **house** cannot stand.

John 14:2
In My Father's **house** are many mansions; if it were not so, I would have told you. I go to prepare a place for you.

I Timothy 3:4
...one who rules his **house** well, having his children in submission in all reverence.

INHERITING THE LAND

Genesis 12:1-2
Now the Lord said to Abram: "Get out of your country from your family and from your father's house, to a **land** that I will show you. I will make you a great nation; I will bless you and make your name great; and you shall be a blessing."

Genesis 12:7
Then the Lord appeared to Abram and said, "To your descendants I will give this **land**." And there he built an altar to the Lord, who had appeared to him.

Genesis 13:9
Is not the whole **land** before you? Please separate from me. If you take the left, I will go right; or, if you go to the right, then I will go to the left.

Genesis 13:17
Arise, walk in the **land** through its length and its width, for I give it to you.

Genesis 15:7
Then He said to him, "I am the Lord, who brought you out of Ur of the Chaldeans, to give you this **land** to inherit it."

Genesis 15:18
On the same day the Lord made a covenant with Abram, saying: "To your descendants I have given this **land**, from the river of Egypt to

the great river, the River Euphrates...."

Genesis 17:8
Also I give to you and your descendants after you the **land** in which you are a stranger, all the **land** of Canaan, as an everlasting possession; and I will be their God.

Genesis 26:2-4
Then the Lord appeared to him (Isaac) and said: "Do not go down to Egypt; live in the **land** of which I shall tell you. Dwell in this **land** and I will be with you and bless you; for to you and your descendants I give all these **lands**, and I will perform the oath which I swore to Abraham your father. And I will make your descendants multiply as the stars of heaven; I will give to your descendants all these **lands**; and in your seed all the nations of the earth shall be blessed...."

Exodus 3:8
So I have come down to deliver them out of the hand of the Egyptians, and to bring them up from that **land** to a good and large **land**, to a land flowing with milk and honey....

Exodus 6:8
And I will bring you into the **land** which I swore to give to Abraham, Isaac, and Jacob; and I will give it to you as a heritage: I am the Lord.

Numbers 32:22
...and the **land** is subdued before the Lord, then afterward you may return and be blameless before the Lord and before Israel; and this **land** shall be your possession before the Lord.

Deuteronomy 1:8
See, I have set the **land** before you; go in and possess the **land** which the Lord swore to your fathers....

Deuteronomy 31:7
Then Moses called Joshua and said to him in the sight of all Israel,

"Be strong and of good courage, for you must go with this people to the **land** which the Lord has sworn to their fathers to give them, and you shall cause them to inherit it."

DOORS AND WINDOWS

Genesis 7:11
...all the fountains of the great deep were broken up and the **windows** of heaven were opened.

Psalm 78:23
Yet He had commanded the clouds above, and opened the **doors** of heaven, had rained down manna on them to eat, and given them the bread of heaven.

Revelation 3:20
Behold, I stand at the **door** and knock. If anyone hears My voice and opens the **door**, I will come in to him and dine with him, and he with me....

Isaiah 24:18
...for the **windows** from on high are open, and the foundations of the earth are shaken.

Isaiah 54:12
I will make your **windows** of rubies, your gates of crystal and all your walls of precious stones.

FOUNDATIONS

Ezra 3:10
When the builders laid the **foundation** of the temple of the Lord, the priests stood in their apparel with trumpets...to praise the Lord, according to the ordinance of David king of Israel.

Ezra 3:11
...then all the people shouted with a great shout, when they praised

the LORD, because the **foundation** of the house of the LORD was laid.

Ezra 6:3
In the first year of King Cyrus, King Cyrus issued a decree concerning the house of God at Jerusalem: "Let the house be rebuilt, the place where they offered sacrifices; and let the **foundations** of it be firmly laid...."

Psalm 87:1
His **foundation** is in the holy mountains. The Lord loves the gates of Zion more than all the dwellings of Jacob.

Psalm 102:25
Of old You laid the **foundation** of the earth, and the heavens are the work of Your hands.

Proverbs 10:25
When the whirlwind passes by, the wicked is no more, but the righteous has an everlasting **foundation**.

Isaiah 28:16
...thus says the Lord God: "Behold, I lay in Zion a stone for a **foundation**, a tried stone, a precious cornerstone, a sure **foundation**."

Isaiah 58:12
Those from among you shall build the old waste places; you shall raise up the **foundations** of many generations....

Luke 6:48
He is like a man building a house, who dug deep and laid the **foundation** on the rock. And when the flood arose, the stream beat vehemently against that house, and could not shake it, for it was founded on the rock.

I Corinthians 3:10-11

According to the grace of God which was given to me, as a wise master builder I have laid the **foundation**, and another builds on it. But let each one take heed how he builds on it. For no other **foundation** can anyone lay than that which is laid, which is Jesus Christ.

Ephesians 1:4

...He chose us in Him before the **foundation** of the world, that we should be holy and without blame before Him in love.

TO BUILD

Numbers 32:24

(God speaking through Moses): "**Build** cities for your little ones and folds for your sheep, and do what has proceeded out of your mouth."

I Samuel 2:35

Then I will raise up for Myself a faithful priest who shall do according to what is in My heart and in My mind. I will **build** him a sure house, and he shall walk before My anointed forever.

2 Samuel 7:13

He shall **build** a house for My name, and I will establish the throne of his kingdom forever.

I Kings 2:36

Then the king sent and called for Shimei, and said to him, "**Build** yourself a house in Jerusalem and dwell there, and do not go out from there anywhere."

I Kings 5:5

And behold, I propose to **build** a house for the name of the Lord my God, as the Lord spoke to my father David, saying, "Your son, whom I will set on your throne in your place, he shall **build** the house for My name."

2 Chronicles 8:1-2
It came to pass at the end of twenty years, when Solomon had **built** the house of the Lord and his own house that the cities which Hiram had given to Solomon, Solomon **built** them; and he settled the children of Israel there.

2 Chronicles 8:4-6
He (Solomon) also **built** Tadmor in the wilderness, and all the storage cities which he **built** in Hamath. He **built** Upper Beth Horon and Lower Beth Horon, fortified cities with walls, gates and bars; ...and all that Solomon desired to **build** in Jerusalem, in Lebanon and in all the land of his dominion.

2 Chronicles 14:6-7
And he (Asa) **built** fortified cities in Judah, for the land had rest; he had no war in those years, because the Lord had given him rest. Therefore he said to Judah, "Let us **build** these cities and make walls around them and towers, gates and bars, while the land is yet before us, because we have sought the Lord our God; we have sought Him, and He has given us rest on every side." So they **built** and prospered.

Ezra 5:2
So Zerubbabel the son of Shealtiel and Jeshua the son of Jozadak rose up and began to **build** the house of God which is in Jerusalem; and the prophets of God were with them, helping them.

Psalm 69:35
For God will save Zion and **build** the cities of Judah, that they may dwell there and possess it.

Psalm 127:1
Unless the Lord **builds** a house, they labor in vain who **build** it.

Proverbs 24:27
Prepare your outside work, make it fit for yourself in the field; and afterward **build** your house.

Isaiah 45:13

"I have raised him up in righteousness, and I will direct all his ways; He shall **build** My city and let My exiles go free, not for price nor reward," says the Lord of hosts.

Isaiah 58:12

Those from among you shall **build** the old waste places; you shall raise up the foundations of many generations....

Isaiah 65:21

They shall **build** houses and inhabit them; they shall plant vineyards and eat their fruit.

Daniel 9:25

...to restore and **build** Jerusalem until Messiah the Prince, there shall be seven weeks and sixty-two weeks; the street shall be **built** again, and the wall, even in troublesome times.

I Corinthians 3:10-11

According to the grace of God which was given to me, as a wise master **builder** I have laid the foundation, and another **builds** on it. But let each one take heed how he **builds** on it. For no other foundation can anyone lay than that which is laid, which is Jesus Christ.

RENEWING YOUR MIND

Romans 12:1, 2

I beseech you therefore, brethren, by the mercies of God, that you present your bodies a living sacrifice, holy acceptable to God, which is your reasonable service. And do not be conformed to this world, but be transformed by the **renewing of your mind**, that you may prove what is that good and acceptable and perfect will of God.

Philippians 2:5

Let this **mind** be in you which was also in Christ Jesus.

I Corinthians 2:9,10,16
But as it is written: "Eye has not seen, nor ear heard, nor have entered into the heart of man the things which God has prepared for those who love Him." But God has revealed them to us through His Spirit. For the Spirit searches all things, yes, the deep things of God. For who has known the mind of the Lord that he may instruct him? But we have the **mind** of Christ.

Ephesians 4:23, 24
And be **renewed in the spirit of your mind**, and that you put on the new man which was created according to God, in true righteousness and holiness.

BUILDING YOUR FAITH TO BELIEVE FOR HOUSES AND LAND

Hebrews 11:1
Now **faith** is the substance of things hoped for, the evidence of things not seen.

Romans 10:17
So then **faith** comes by hearing, and hearing by the word of God.

Mark 11:22-24
So Jesus answered and said to them, "Have **faith** in God. For assuredly, I say to you, whoever says to this mountain, 'Be removed and be cast into the sea,' and does not doubt in his heart, but **believes that those things he says will be done**, he will have whatever he says. Therefore I say to you, whatever things you ask **when you pray, believe that you receive them, and you will have them.**"

Philippians 4:13
I can do all things through Christ who strengthens me.

NOTES:

NOTES:

NOTES:

NOTES:

NOTES:

NOTES:

NOTES:

NOTES:

NOTES:

NOTES:

NOTES:

NOTES:

Printed in the United States
85568LV00006B/86/A

9 781933 141039